An Actor Prepares...

to Work in New York City

A STEP-BY-STEP GUIDE
TO LAUNCHING
A CAREER IN
THE BIG APPLE

LIMELIGHT EDITIONS
NEW YORK

An Actor Prepares...

to Work in New York City

*How to Master
the Business of
"The Business"*

WITHDRAWN

Craig Wroe

First Limelight Edition July 2004

Published in the United States by Limelight Editions

Interior design and typesetting by Rachel Reiss

Manufactured in the United States of America

LIBRARY OF CONGRESS CATALOGING-IN-PUBLICATION DATA
Wroe, Craig.
   An actor prepares—to work in New York City : how to master the business of the business : a step-by-step guide for actors to launching a career in the Big Apple / Craig Wroe.—1st Limelight ed.
      p. cm.
   Includes index.
   ISBN 0-87910-306-X (pbk.)
   1. Acting—Vocational guidance—New York (State)—New York.
2. New York
(N.Y.)--Guidebooks. I. Title.
PN2055.W77 2004
792.02'8'0237471--dc22

                                                            2004014356

For
Mark Hammer
and
Joan Mazzarelli

Acknowledgments

I dedicate this book to my grandmother Joan Mazzarelli, whose life and love are a constant inspiration, and to my grad school teacher and adviser, Mark Hammer, whose influence in and impact on my career I feel every day. There isn't a time when I'm either acting or teaching that he's not sitting on my shoulder, inspiring me to "be better."

I offer mountains of appreciation to the many friends and colleagues who contributed ideas, anecdotes and inspiration. Special thanks to Jacqueline Farrington, Henny Russell, John Ryan, Frank Rizzo, John Wojda, Dea Lawrence, Lisa Tatham, Conan McCarty, Andrea Pollak, Ellen Ferris, Chuck Morey, Michael Gregory, Shelley Delaney, Rosalyn Coleman-Williams, Craig Williams, Chris Downey, Patrick Frederic, Maggie Frederic, Michael Chaban, Dennis Delaney, Bill Kux, Reno Roop, Pat Fraser, Laurine Towler, Andrea Cirie, Dontonio Davis, Buzz Roddy, Daniel Agatino, Davis Melendez, Alexandra Hartley-Leonard and Farin Chasin.

Thanks also to my copy editor Nina Maynard, whose prowess with a red pen once again amazes, and to artists Annette Berry and Johanna Goodman for the wonderful work they did on the cover.

Kudos to my literary agent Maura Teitelbaum, the best agent a writer could ask for, and to her assistants Samantha Ryan and David Shah for helping to make my life a little easier.

Buckets of gratitude go out to my legit agents Mary Harden, Nancy Curtis, Michael Kirsten, Scott Edwards, Nancy Leier and Diane Riley for their years of support and friendship, and for teaching me most of what I know about "the business." Ditto that sentiment to Tracy Goldblum, Genine Esposito, Alison Quartin and the entire crew in the Commercial Department at Abrams Artists.

Thanks to everyone at Amadeus Press/Limelight Editions, especially Jenna Young for being so meticulous and Rachel Reiss for the great design work.

Thanks also to all of the organizations and businesses and their representatives who helped make this book as comprehensive as possible, including Elba Aviles at AFTRA, Marjorie Murray Roop at The Actors' Fund of America, Actors' Equity Association Business Representative Valerie LaVacco, Patricia S. Schwadron at the Actors' Work Program, Gary Ginsberg at Royal Alliance, actors' accountant Marc Bernstein, Ellen Celnik at Common Ground Management (who oversees The Aurora apartment complex), Yossi Fabor of the Al Hirschfeld Free Health Clinic, Secretary Treasurer of Actors' Equity Association and Coordinator of VITA site 35006 Conard Fowkes, The Actors' Fund of America, Actors' Equity Association, Screen Actors Guild and American Federation of Television and Radio Artists.

There are roughly three New Yorks. There is first, the New York of the man or woman who was born here, who takes the city for granted and accepts its size and its turbulence as natural and inevitable. Second, there is the New York of the commuter—the city that is devoured by locusts each day and spat out each night. Third, there is the New York of the person who was born somewhere else and came to New York in quest of something. Of these three trembling cities the greatest is the last—the city of final destination, the city that is a goal. It is this third city that accounts for New York's high-strung disposition, its poetical deportment, its dedication to the arts, and its incomparable achievements. Commuters give the city its tidal restlessness; natives give it solidity and continuity; but the settlers give it passion. And whether it is a farmer arriving from Italy to set up a small grocery store in a slum, or a young girl arriving from a small town in Mississippi to escape the indignity of being observed by her neighbors, or a boy arriving from the Corn Belt with a manuscript in his suitcase and pain in his heart, it makes no difference: each embraces New York with the intense excitement of first love, each absorbs New York with the fresh eyes of an adventurer, each generates heat and light to dwarf the Consolidated Edison Company.

—E.B. WHITE, *HERE IS NEW YORK*

I have learned this at least by my experiment: that if one advances confidently in the direction of his dreams, and endeavors to live the life which he has imagined, he will meet with success unexpected in common hours.

—HENRY DAVID THOREAU, *WALDEN*

Never meddle with play-actors, for they're a favored race.
—MIGUEL DE CERVANTES, *DON QUIXOTE*

Key of Acronyms Used in Text

ACFCU = Artists Community Federal Credit Union
AEA = Actors' Equity Association (Equity)
AFCU = Actors Federal Credit Union
AFM = American Federation of Musicians
AFTRA = American Federation of Television and Radio Artists
AGMA = American Guild of Musical Artists
AGVA = American Guild of Variety Artists
AHIRC = Artist's Health Insurance Resource Center
AMMI = American Museum of the Moving Image
APD = Academy Players Directory
AWP = Actors' Work Program
BC/EFA = Broadway Cares/Equity Fights AIDS
CSA = Casting Society of America
CTFD = Career Transition for Dancers
DGA = Directors Guild of America
GIAA = Guild of Italian American Actors
HOLA = Hispanic Organization of Latin Actors
IATSE = International Alliance of Theatrical Stage Employees
IMDB = Internet Movie Database
ISP = Internet Service Provider

NABET = National Association of Broadcast Employees and Technicians
NATR = National Association of Talent Representatives
NTCP = Non-Traditional Casting Project
NYPL = New York Public Library
NYT = The New York Times
PGNY = Players' Guide New York
SAG = Screen Actors Guild
SSDC = Society of Stage Directors and Choreographers
TCG = Theater Communications Group
TDF = Theater Development Fund
UMDN = Union Members Discount Network
VASTA = Voice and Speech Trainers Association
VITA = Volunteer Income Tax Assistance
WGA = Writers Guild of America

Contents

Helluva Town

Life upon the wicked stage ain't nothin' what a girl supposes...
JEROME KERN, *SHOWBOAT*

Ever wonder why we are actors? Is it that we like showing off? Wearing costumes? The paycheck (as paltry as it sometimes is)? The parties? Sleeping in? Not punching a time clock? The free food on opening nights? Sure, all those things are great, but for most of us, we do it because it gives us a lot of pleasure. Every actor I know, myself included, acts because there's no greater feeling, no greater rush than working on a stage in front of an audience or in a studio in front of a camera, bringing a character to life. Moreover, most of us answer the "Why are you an actor" question with this same retort: "There is nothing else I can or want to do." For most actors, acting is a calling...we don't choose it so much as it chooses us. It's something we *have* to do. Unfortunately, we don't always get to do it. Given the competition, the economy and scarcity of roles, unemployment is the rule and work the exception.

Being an actor anywhere is not an easy proposition. Being an actor in New York City is next to impossible. This crazy place, where some come to pursue stardom, some anonymity and others everything in between, is unarguably one of the toughest and roughest cities in the industrialized world.

The clichés about the city are true: it's crowded, noisy, filthy, insanely paced, malodorous in summer, clammy and cold in winter. It's rude, crude, impersonal and in-your-face twenty-four/seven. And cost? Fuhgedaboutit! It takes a fortune to breathe here: rents are obscene (good luck finding that elusive "decent," affordable apartment) and the price of most everything else is out of control. The city can drain our savings, pull our focus, sap our energy and steal our souls if we're not attentive. It's no place for sensitive (not to mention starving) artist types.

Speaking of artists, we could not have chosen a more difficult profession. When I told a friend that I was writing a guide for actors who are moving to New York City to pursue their dreams, he glibly replied, "What more can you tell them except, 'Say your prayers every night and plan to skip lots of meals'?" Much truth is said in jest. The life of an actor, which invariably includes rejection, stretches of unemployment and lots of self-doubt, can be cruel, trying, lonely, impoverished, and spiritually and physically exhausting. And competitive (go figure!): A recent study revealed that, at any given time, there are 90,000 people in this city who call themselves actors. Of those actors, a number slightly less than 2000 are working at any given time, which means there are 88,000 actors out there who are unemployed. There are 88,000 actors out there looking for work. There are 87,999 actors out there who are competing with you to get the attention of agents, casting directors, producers and directors. No one fresh off the boat, bus, plane and train who has come to be a New York actor can help but experience the dreaded double whammy epiphany: tough city; tougher career.

Have I spooked you? Actually, the city isn't nearly as bleak as the picture I've painted. It wouldn't be one of the world's most populous urban centers if it were. It wouldn't be the center of the universe (I'm just a little jingoistic) if it were. Indeed, a lot of the negatives I've listed are the things about the city that one comes to love after the bumpy honeymoon, and that energize, electrify and give it its edge. As I say in *An Actor Prepares . . . To Live in New York City:*

> For anyone in the performing arts, this is the place to be. No
> other city has the diversity and quality of live theater, dance

and music that we have here in the Big Apple. No other city can boast the numbers of resources, organizations, services, unions, guilds and training institutions that are available to us here. For those actors who are just starting out, there's no better base from which to launch a career. For those who have been working in other parts of the country, New York is the inevitable next rung up the career ladder.

So, how do you launch a career in New York? How do you climb that ladder? How do you make your mark?

Of course, talent and training are first and foremost. You have to be ready. You have to know how to act, how to create a character, how to be truthful and interesting. You have to have the goods, know what you're doing and know how to deliver. By the time you arrive here, you should have trained (or plan to train) rigorously; your skills should be honed and your craft perfected.

After talent and training, you'll need to have a very clear understanding of how "the business" works and then apply that knowledge to getting ahead in a crowded field. It is my firm belief that each of us has to take control of our own careers. We must mentor our careers. The analogy I like to use is based on a business model: our careers are our corporations and we are president, CEO, CFO and chairman of the board. It is up to us to grow our corporation from a small "ma and pa" operation to a thriving, healthy Fortune 500 conglomerate. To do that, we need to know "the business" inside and out. We need to be experts on everything from pictures and resumes to agents, casting directors, mailings, publicity, unions, training, auditions, connections and actor resources, and how each can be utilized to help us achieve our dreams.

My purpose in this book is to give you the necessary tools to help you transition from newcomer to New Yorker, from neophyte to working actor. Drawn from my own experiences as well as those of scores of friends and colleagues, the information in this book will give you most everything you'll need to know to master the business of "the business." The road isn't an easy one—there will be sleepless nights, hungry days and tons of frustration. You'll have to summon up endless reserves of energy, drive, commitment and gumption. However difficult though, the reward is sweet: a career in the greatest profession in the world, in the greatest city in the world.

"Zone
of
Comfortability"

Welcome to New York

So, you've just arrived in the city and are the next Meryl Streep or Johnny Depp waiting to be discovered. Where do you start? First things first—get here and get settled. Really settled. Create for yourself what I call a "zone of comfortability." Find a home for yourself, get your life in order, take care of your external needs, and get *comfortable*, so that when it comes time to pursue your career, you are able to devote all your energy and concentration to that end and not be distracted.

The impetus for writing both this and my previous book came out of recognizing this need. I witnessed a lot of my students, friends and colleagues floundering, trying to set up a home, have a social life, juggle their acting careers with survival jobs, and live here with a modicum of ease. They were spinning their wheels and ultimately burning out before their careers got started. Thus, I devised the "zone."

My recommendations for creating the "zone of comfortability" are as follows:

Arrive with money . . . Don't come to the city empty-handed. Have at your disposal as much money as you can muster and be careful how you spend it once you arrive. New York is outrageously expensive—it's not unheard of to blow a wad of cash on "life" things and at the end of the day wind up with nothing to show for it. You'll need money for your apartment, which often includes both first and last month's rent, a security deposit, a "key" deposit (basically a tip to the landlord or superintendent of a building for handing over the keys . . . a shady practice but one that nonetheless occurs a lot), and a broker's fee, which can be several thousands of dollars; setting-up-home costs (furniture, housewares, utilities, telephone, cable, internet service provider, health club, etc.); and incidental fees that can be downright extortionate. A thick cushion of cash can help buffer the blow when you start laying it out.

Find a financial institution where you can deposit that thick cushion of cash . . . You'll want to do your research to find a bank that will give you decent interest rates and low- or no-fee checking—not an easy prospect in the Big Apple (make sure to bring two forms of identification). For a lot of actors, the favored alternatives to banks are credit unions (nonprofit institutions owned and controlled by those who use them). Credit union interest rates are usually more stable, checking is free, the service is usually more personal and personable, and members are offered special deals as well as lower rates on loans, mortgages, credit cards and other services:

The **Actors Federal Credit Union (AFCU)**, a cooperatively run, nonprofit banking organization, was chartered in 1962 to serve the entertainment community. Any paid-up member of Equity, AFTRA and SAG in good standing, or member of a component organization is eligible to apply for membership. The myriad benefits for members of the AFCU include:
- Two convenient office locations:
  165 West 46th Street (Actors Equity Building), 14th Floor—
    212-869-8926
  322 West 48th (Musicians Local Building), 4th Floor
  www.actorsfcu.com
- Interest and dividend rates that are competitive with or better than commercial or savings banks
- Federally insured deposits up to $100,000 by the National Credit Union Association

- Free checking with overdraft protection for accounts that maintain an average daily balance of $99
- Two types of overdraft protection: automatic loan from Cash Draw or automatic transfer from regular savings
- Actorcash (isn't that an oxymoron?) ATM Cards which can be used to access cash from both savings and checking accounts at ATMs worldwide. (I know this is true—I've used my Actorcash ATM Card in Mexico, Hungary, Italy, the Netherlands, France, United Kingdom and Austria and have never had a problem.) Actorcash ATM Cards can be used to make purchases at many stores. Via the CO-OP network, members can make deposits and withdrawals without being surcharged at participating ATMs across the country.
- Actors Gold and Classic Visa Cards with a 6.9 percent introductory rate and an 11.9 percent fixed rate (well below the typical 17 to 23 percent rates of most commercial banks) with no annual fees and a twenty-five–day grace period. Actors Visa benefits include access to cash at ATM machines worldwide, free travel accident insurance, auto rental insurance, ninety-day purchase protection and extended warranties.
- ActorMiles MasterCard—which allows members to earn credit toward free airline tickets throughout the United States and much of Europe with every purchase
- Free investment counseling with financial consultants to help you obtain your long- and short-term financial goals. Through mutual funds, fixed and variable annuities, and tax-free and tax-deferred investments, the AFCU will help create a comprehensive investment package that is right for you.
- Touch-tone Teller services—from the convenience of a phone, you may check your balances and cleared checks, transfer funds and make loan payments.
- Free full-service banking via the internet (www.actorsfcu.com) allows members to pay bills, check balances and account his-

tories, apply for loans, transfer balances within accounts and view a complete listing of current rates and services online.

- Regular savings accounts
- Individual Retirement Accounts
- Low mortgage rates
- Payroll deduction for direct deposit
- Deposit by mail
- Low auto loan rates and an annual auto sale in which participating auto dealers nationwide offer members the lowest possible prices on their inventories, thus eliminating the need to haggle over pricing
- Personal loans with rates lower than major New York banks and no prepayment penalty if you repay the loan before it is due
- Free life insurance, which matches the amount you have on deposit at the time of death, up to $5,000
- Wire transfers
- Gift check, money orders and travelers checks
- US Savings Bond redemption
- Free notary service
- Unlimited internet access for only $9.95 per month with the first month free, including four e-mail accounts, 24/7 technical support and up to 20 mb of web space. (See chapter on "Internet Service Providers.")
- The ability to make safe and secure cash and check deposits at several check cashing offices throughout Manhattan, Brooklyn, Bronx and Queens. This service offers members the convenience of multiple locations as well as weekend service and extended hours of access (as early as 8 A.M., as late as 7 P.M.). Unlike traditional ATMs, funds deposited at these locations are immediately available for withdrawal.
- Over 115 fee-free ATMs located throughout the city, with plans for the installation of several more in the near future.

Call or go by either of the Actors Federal Credit Union offices for a complete list of ATM outlets.
• Online bill payment
For years I resisted the exhortations of friends and colleagues to join the AFCU. Not that I'm stubborn or anything, but it was hard for me to comprehend that the credit union could be as safe and dependable as a commercial bank. It was only after wretched experiences at three of the New York banking behemoths that I decided to give the AFCU a try. I still kick myself for the years I wasted and the money I lost banking with the big boys. It's a no-brainer, with enormous benefits, competitive interest rates and excellent service (not to mention our money stays in the "family" so to speak). There is no better place for actors to bank than the AFCU.

The **Artists Community Federal Credit Union (ACFCU)** (351-A West 54th Street—212-246-3344, www.artistscommunityfcu.org), a federally insured financial cooperative that is owned and controlled by its members, offers an array of financial services to artists, art workers and non-profit arts organizations in New York. Services include:
• Checking accounts with no or low monthly fees and competitive interest rates
• ATM cards that can be used in network at no cost, or out of network for a small transaction fee
• Savings/Money Market accounts with competitive interest rates
• Certificates of Deposit (CDs) investment for set periods at fixed interest rates that are competitive with those of traditional banks
• IRAs available for new deposits and for transfers from other institutions

- Loans secured by government contracts, grants, commissions, performance contracts and deposits in the credit union are available to both individuals and non-profit arts groups.
- Unsecured loans are available to individuals, but at higher interest rates.
- Members receive monthly checking account statements and quarterly savings account statements.
- All deposits are federally insured up to $100,000 by the National Credit Union Administration (NCUA).

Any type of artist is eligible to join the ACFCU, including painters, musicians, writers, actors, filmmakers, photographers, dancers and more. To join, call to set up an appointment. The ACFCU requires a $100 minimum to open a savings account; $500 for a Money Market account; $1000 for a CD or IRA; and a $500 balance is necessary for checking if you want to avoid a $7.50 monthly service charge. When you join, you'll be required to pay a one-time membership fee of $10.

Find an affordable home . . . Be prepared—this is, as I'm sure you know, a near impossible task. For the tireless, however, it is not insurmountable: Ask everyone you know if they have heard about a vacant apartment; check bulletin boards at the unions and other places you frequent; think seriously about living in one of the city's other boroughs or in New Jersey; check out the great community-based website www.craigslist.com daily for listings; consider living with a roommate—someone who either already has an apartment or with whom you can look together for something; check out the "Apartments for Rent" sections in local newspapers, especially the *Village Voice.* I recommend strongly against subletting, as you'll be living in someone else's space, with someone else's things. The idea of creating a "zone of comfortability" is for you to be in your own space, amidst your own belongings.

There is an outlet where actors can go for help in finding a New York City home and a number of residences designated for performing artists. These include:

The Actors' Fund of America (729 Seventh Avenue at 49th Street—212-221-7300, ext. 257, www.actorsfund.org) knows almost everything there is to know about affordable housing in the city and will be happy to assist you in your search. They will answer your questions about the 80/20 lottery (buildings in which 20 percent of the tenants are in the low-income category—these are usually new buildings that get tax breaks for providing this kind of housing), and give you an updated list of 80/20 buildings to write to for applications. They also have a complete list of New York City buildings like Manhattan Plaza, The Aurora and Times Square Apartments (discussed below), where you may write to request a place on their waiting lists. The Fund can also help answer inquiries regarding the Section 8 Housing Assistance Program subsidy, including eligibility, apartment availability, and the application process. When you call The Actors Fund, sign up for their monthly "Affordable Housing" seminars and request a copy of their housing information packet that gives a comprehensive overview of the things you need to know in your search for a New York City home. The Actors' Fund of America receives a high volume of calls regarding housing questions, but if you leave a message they will eventually return your call.

The Aurora located at 475 West 57th Street and Tenth Avenue in midtown is a thirty-story building that provides affordable, supportive housing to special low-income groups, such as seniors, performing arts professionals and people living with HIV/AIDS. Originally intended to be a luxury high-rise, The Aurora was converted into 178 "shared" residential units. This means that each resident has his/her own bedroom unit but shares a living room and kitchen with one or two roommates. Some units share a bathroom with one other person; some have a private bath within the bedroom unit. Twenty-seven one-bedroom units serve eligible individuals who have special medical needs.

Eligibility for the building is based on federal guidelines under the Internal Revenue Service Federal Tax Credit Program: A person's annual income from all sources may not exceed $23,500 and should not be less than $13,000. Households of two may apply for a one bedroom if both members are persons with AIDS or are senior citizens with joint incomes not exceeding $27,000 annually or less than $14,000. To apply, contact:

Intake Department/Common Ground Management
475 West 57th Street, 4th Floor
New York, NY 10019
212-262-4502

Known as "The Miracle on 42nd Street," **Manhattan Plaza** is one of the most unique residential complexes anywhere. Built in 1977, Manhattan Plaza was intended to be a luxury condominium building stretching a full city block from Ninth to Tenth Avenues, between 42nd and 43rd Streets. As the project neared completion however, the builder filed for bankruptcy protection. Worse, the neighborhood was still considered to be "in transition," meaning no one who could afford a luxury apartment wanted to live in Hell's Kitchen. After an intensive effort on the part of city officials, performing artists and unions, Broadway producers and civic leaders, the U.S. Department of Housing and Urban Development designated Manhattan Plaza eligible to receive a Section 8 Housing Assistance Program subsidy.

The idea behind Manhattan Plaza was to create a community for those who could not otherwise afford to live right in the heart of the theater district. With the federal rent subsidy, performers were offered a chance to live where they "plied their trades," and the elderly and people who had made the area their home for many years were able to stay, helping the neighborhood to retain its character and diversity.

Created as an experiment in housing and performing arts support, almost from the day the first tenant moved in, Manhattan Plaza became the prime catalyst in the redevelopment and preservation of the Westside. It has brought thousands of hard-working, energetic people back into Clinton/Hell's Kitchen and generated a host of commercial establishments, such as theaters, bars, restaurants, cafes, markets, specialty gift shops and bakeries.

Today, roughly 70 percent of Manhattan Plaza's residents earn their living in the performing arts as actors, dancers, directors, writers, singers, technicians, ushers, theater managers or designers. The remaining 30 percent are the elderly, handicapped and long-term neighborhood residents. Approximately 90 percent of the tenants receive some federal rent subsidy (under the Section 8 program, residents are obligated to pay 30 percent of their annual income to rent, with the federal government making up the difference); the remaining 10 percent pay "fair market" rent.

As you can imagine, the desire to live at Manhattan Plaza is great. As you can also imagine, getting in is next to impossible. Because the waiting list is years-long, it is often closed to new applications. I waited (yeah, I'm a resident) four years; a friend of mine who moved in this year waited seven years. Only infrequently does the list open to new applicants; when it does, it is usually announced in the trade paper *Backstage* or in *Equity News*. If you see that the list has opened, it will only be so for a few days and may not open again for years, so act immediately. You can also write Manhattan Plaza to ask for notification of the list openings and for the eligibility requirements for residing there:

Manhattan Plaza Business Office
400 West 43rd Street
New York, NY 10036

The **Times Square** residential complex is a small-scale version of Manhattan Plaza. It is also a Section 8 Housing Assistance Program building in the heart of the theater district and has several apartments designated for performing artists. The Times Square differs in size (only 650 units) from Manhattan Plaza and has a much shorter waiting list to get in (about six months). To be eligible, you must be a single adult with a yearly income between $12,000 and $26,400. If you meet these criteria, call and request an application. The apartments are tiny—basically one room half the size of an average bedroom that serves as kitchen, sleeping, living and dining room (fortunately, each room has a decent-size bathroom). About all that can fit are a single bed, dresser, small bookshelf, television, table and chair. The pullman kitchen is not great if you love to cook or entertain (not that you could in this small room, unless you had your guests line up in the hallway and come in one at a time): there are two burners, a dormitory-size refrigerator and no oven. Despite these drawbacks, the Times Square apartments provide a safe home in the center of midtown, an affordable rent, and a place to hang your hat while you are pursuing your career and hunting for a bigger place to live. Contact the Times Square office at:

255 West 43rd Street
New York, NY 10036
Phone: 212-768-8989, ext. 2018

Set up your new home . . . Unpack. Send out your change of address notices. Have the utilities turned on and cable and telephone hooked up. Buy a bed, some furniture and arrange it. Hang a few pictures. Get some cookware, plates, cups, and utensils; stock your refrigerator.

Create a budget and stick to it . . . Don't overuse your credit cards and don't buy anything unless you can really afford it. I can't tell you how many of my actor friends are dealing with crippling debt because they went hog-wild with their credit cards, or arrived here with astronomical student loan and/or moving debt, and then heaped living-in-New-York debt on top of it. Many of them have had to forego their careers to pay off their bills.

Flummoxed as to how to stick to a budget in this expensive city? Do your research. Don't buy at the first place you go to. Snoop around, do comparison-shopping, and ask friends where the bargains are. With some extra effort, you can find the best groceries, goods and services for less.

The best way to create a budget is to make a chart listing all your monthly bills—rent, utilities, phone, cell phone, credit cards (the maximum you're willing to pay each month), groceries, entertainment, and incidentals. Add each together to determine what the minimum is you need to make each month to pay for these. At the end of the month, subtract that predetermined number from the total amount of money you have in all accounts. Then add that resulting figure to the amount you made that month. This total should be what you end up with in your accounts at the end of the month. If you have less, you've gone over your budget and you'll have to be more diligent the following month.

Confused? Here's an example:

First, determine your monthly expenses:

MONTHLY BUDGET—EXPENSES

Rent	$ 995.00
Utilities	$ 65.00
Phone	$ 36.00
Cell phone	$ 48.58
Long Distance	$ 32.00
Cable	$ 45.00
American Express	$ 100.00
Visa	$ 100.00
Food/Entertainment/Incidentals	$ 565.00
Internet Service Provider	$ 21.95
Total	**$ 2008.53**

Your total monthly nut is $2008.53. You know you have to make that much to break even.

Now, total up everything you made that month, for example:

MONTHLY INCOME

Waiting tables (salary and tips)	$ 2090.00
Film extra work	$ 320.00
Guest star on Law and Order (one day)	$ 850.00
Babysitting	$ 120.00
Total	**$ 3380.00**

The total income you've made in that month is $3,380.00.

Now deduct your expenses from your income:

Income	$3380.00
Expenses	-$2008.53
Total	**$ 1371.47**

$1371.47 is how much extra you should have left over (surplus cash) after all expenses. (Of course, if there are large unforeseen expenses like medical bills, photo reproduction, coaching fees for an audition, etc., add those to the "Expenses" column and then also deduct that total from your "Income.")

Take that total and add it to what you have in the bank:

Income	$3380.00
Less expenses	-$2008.53
Less other expenses	-$ 402.00
Surplus Cash	$ 969.47
Amount in Bank Accounts	$2657.13
Total Assets at the end of month	**$ 3626.60**

You should have $3,626.60 in your bank account at the end of the month. If you have anything less, you've gone over your budget.

Since you are the "CEO" of your own corporation, you'll need an office . . . Find a room, corner, hallway or closet in your apartment that you can designate as your workspace. It is from here that you will be launching your career. Try each day to spend some time in this space focusing on the things you need to do to become a successful actor. Make sure that your office is comfortable, clean, well lighted and inviting so that you'll actually look forward to spending time there.

All good CEOs understand the important contribution 21st century technology makes to the success of their companies. You should too. **If you don't already own a computer and printer, buy both as soon as possible.** They are probably the most valuable technological investments of your career and are tax write-offs, to boot. Owning a computer and printer is almost as important as owning a phone. Not only do they allow actors to communicate with the world via e-mail, but they can also be our most valuable marketing tools. With both, we can create our acting resumes (and update them), stationery, press releases, mass mailings and mail merges, agent queries, business cards and address books. We can download plays via the internet; research playwrights, actors, directors, theaters, classes; obtain information on repertory seasons for theaters both in and around the New York area and throughout the country; join online acting communities; create a personal website; and even receive audition sides. (Tip: When purchasing a computer, think seriously about getting a laptop—you can lug it effortlessly to wherever your career leads you.)

Also, if you don't already have one, **seriously consider getting a cell phone.** Cell phones are practically indispensable to actors. They provide a fail-safe way for directors, agents, producers and casting people to contact us, especially for last-minute appointments. Also, since our work often takes us out of town, cellular service is the best way to keep in touch with friends, family and business contacts.

Other technological tools you should think about owning include an **answering machine** for when you receive work-related calls at home; a **fax machine** for sending resumes and receiving sides; and a **scanner** so that you may scan your picture into your computer for use on stationery or to send to casting people via e-mail.

You say you're a Luddite and eschew all technology? Get over yourself! The competition is using these tools, shouldn't you? Do you want the edge in your profession or not? If you do, you'll enter the 21st century ("join us, it's painless") and take control of your career.

If you don't want to burn through all that cash you've arrived with, you'll need to find a survival job . . . To be in the "zone," it should be something you can bear. Better yet, try to find work that stimulates you, won't exhaust you and might even present a challenge. What are your hobbies? What are your passions? Can you turn these things into an interesting and exciting job? You are a "creative type," so be creative in what you do to pay the bills.

Whatever it is you do, don't let your survival work interfere with your acting career. If you find a day job that won't let you leave for auditions, what's the point? You're here to act. Conversely, if you have a job that keeps you up until very late at night (waiting, bartending, hosting, tollbooth collector, security guard—you get the point) so that you're too exhausted during the day to go to auditions or do all the things you'll need to do to maintain your career, quit. Again, what's the point? A survival job supports you while you are pursuing your dreams; don't let it supplant your dreams.

If you can't find anything that engages you, at the very least look for a job that will let you out for auditions and other acting-related appointments. If that's impossible, do as one enterprising friend of mine did: find an employer who is too naïve (read, dumb!) to tell when you are dissembling. This friend worked at a major department store for several years, and at least once a week, some small tragedy occurred ("ptomaine poisoning," "burst water pipes at home," "a friend was hit by a cab," "my rash is back and I have to go to the doctor NOW") that would force her to leave work early. She was really dashing to auditions. A caveat: If you're going this route, keep your stories straight, don't repeat mishaps or let them go over the top, and be credible.

Survival jobs can be found through several channels: the classified ads of the city's many newspapers; temporary employment agencies (most of which understand actors' needs and offer flexible schedules); asking friends and colleagues if they know of any available work; and internet job listing sites like www.craigslist.com.

One of the best ways to find survival work is to utilize the services of **The Actors' Work Program** (729 Seventh Avenue, 11th Floor, New York, NY 10019—212-354-5480). This great organization, under the auspices of The Actors' Fund of America, offers free counseling, education and training to help us support ourselves between acting jobs and to develop parallel talents so that our survival work is as challenging and creative as is our chosen profession. Members are encouraged to develop the skills needed (such as computing, teaching, time management, small business practices, interviewing, proofreading, etc.) to secure meaningful remunerative work. The AWP also holds weekly job search seminars and has a continually updated list of available job offerings. To join the AWP, you must be a member of an entertainment industry union and must attend one of their weekly orientation meetings held each Monday from 12:00 noon to 2:30 P.M. (For more information on survival work and The Actors' Work Program, refer to the "Meaningful Interim Work and Career Transition" section of the "Index of Actor Resources and Services" chapter.)

Join a gym... Working out helps us develop the strength and stamina we'll need to pursue our careers, work our survival jobs, have active social lives and become citizens of the city. Working out also makes us look great and is the best way to focus energy, blow off steam, relieve frustrations (we'll have a few), empower us with confidence and stay healthy.

Immerse yourself in the arts and in the world... The cliché that actors are stupid is just, well...stupid. The brightest people I know are all actors. After all, we are called on to play all kinds of characters from all walks of life, periods and centuries. No matter whether we're doing a play by Aeschylus, Shakespeare, Molière, Ibsen, Stoppard or tomorrow's bright new voice, we have to have an in-depth knowledge of the era in which the play takes place if we're going to succeed in convincing an audience and effectively deliver the material. We need to have a comprehensive understanding of the social mores and customs, politics, religion, culture, philosophy and science of each era. We must have a good idea of how the people from each period lived, loved, laughed, walked, talked, thought, ate, slept, interacted, worked and played if we're going to breathe life into these characters on a stage or in front of a camera. Therefore, it is essential for us to read histories, biographies and historical novels. We should also read the newspaper beyond the arts section: we have to know what's going on in the world if we're going to satisfactorily present it.

In addition, attending theater regularly is imperative to our growth as artists and to our careers. We must be familiar with the work of playwrights, directors, actors and designers, many of whom we will no doubt collaborate with at some stage in our careers. The plays that are being done in New York today will be done elsewhere next season, and we will very likely be auditioning for those productions.

Going to the theater, moreover, is a great way to network. Theater professionals, whom you should know and work with, go to the theater all the time. This is a way to meet those people.

Most important, there is much we can learn by watching others work. Viewing good and bad acting is always a learning experience and can both enhance our growth and influence our work. Great acting can be an epiphany, an inspiration, and a standard by which we try to measure our own work. Lazy, mediocre and just plain bad acting can serve to shed light on our own shortcomings, expose the traps of our craft and remind us of how fragile this thing is we do.

The same can be said for film and television. Go to the movies, watch TV, rent videos. Subscribe to cable television. (For some of the ways that actors are eligible to view theater and film either gratis or cheap, see the "Free and Discounted Theater and Film" section of the "Index of Actor Resources and Services.")

Furthermore, immersing ourselves in all of the arts will enhance our own craft and complete our knowledge of the world. Listen to music. See dance. Go to the opera. Attend museums. By scrutinizing drawings, paintings, sculpture, jewelry, artifacts, furniture, fashion and weaponry from any given era, we can learn much about the history, culture and social life of the people of that period. Take advantage of anything and everything that expands your education and contributes to your creative process.

(For a complete guide to apartment hunting, bargain provisions, goods and services, banking institutions, affordable cultural venues, gyms, inexpensive healthcare, cell phone and internet service providers and inexpensive everything else in New York, check out my *Living Smart—New York City: The Ultimate Insider's Guide for the Budget Savvy* . . . Nothin' like a little shameless self-promotion, eh?)

So, you've got your personal life together, you're in the "zone." You have a home, a social life, a bank account, and a budget you're sticking to. You've mastered the computer that lives on the desk in your home office. You're working out three times a week, you're up to your ears in art and culture (and you love it) and you actually have a survival job that you can endure. What do you do now? It's time to start working on that career.

Headshots

Stiff Competition

When trying to "sell" ourselves to the industry, the headshot is our most beneficial marketing tool. It is the equivalent of a calling card and is our initial entry into industry offices. Although it is our talent that we hope to sell, it is how we present ourselves on an 8 x 10 piece of paper that will initially capture the interest and attention of agents, casting directors, directors, and producers. A good headshot (more about this anon) can literally make a career—it can open all the right doors, especially in the beginning of our careers. Conversely, a poor headshot can potentially shut us out. Remember that figure I quoted in the first chapter? At any given time, 90,000 people in New York City call themselves actors, yet only about 2000 are working. That's a lot of people (about 88,000) vying for work, vying for attention. The only way to make a splash is to outshine the others. How do you do that? An outstanding headshot is a good start.

Depending on the kinds of work you will be pursuing, you will need at least a couple of different pictures: the "legit" shot for theater, television and film work, which says, "I'm a good, unique, serious actor" (usually with a closed-mouth smile); and an "I'm warm, friendly, enthusiastic and honest, so trust me when I tell you to buy this" commercial shot (in which you'll want to have a vibrant smile that shows some teeth). For those women who want to work on soap operas, you should have a third picture that makes you look glamorous, sultry, and sexy.

In its function as a calling card, a headshot has to be great if it's going to stand out in our overcrowded field. It has to be so compelling that the powers-that-be will not only want to meet you, they'll need to meet you. What makes an exemplary headshot? One that looks like you (you'll piss a lot of people off if you walk into an audition or meeting looking nothing like your headshot), captures your "type" and personality (for more on this, see the chapter "Take Control"), and shows you at your best—warm, open, attractive, confident, interesting, successful, friendly, a spark in the eyes, comfortable in your own skin, a natural smile, intelligent, well groomed, funny, charming, fun to be with in a rehearsal room or on a set, spontaneous, a good actor. It should be an honest but positive depiction of you in one of your finest moments (not the finest you look, perhaps), and, in the best of all possible worlds, reveal a bit of your soul. To achieve all of these objectives, the talents of a remarkable photographer are required.

Finding a Photographer

The process of finding someone who is creative and comfortable to work with and who will deliver that exemplary headshot can be daunting. It often seems as though there are as many photographers in this city as there are actors. Their ads overwhelm the pages of the trade papers, actor-oriented bulletin boards, and, in some neighborhoods, phone booths and lampposts. With a glut of photographers, how do you determine who is good, who should be avoided, who you will best "click" with and who will wholly capture you?

The most reliable way of finding the ideal photographer is by word of mouth. Poll your actor friends and colleagues for which photographers they have used and whether they are pleased with the results. If you see a headshot you particularly like, ask who did it. Query all industry people you know to find out whom they would suggest; agents, especially, will have ideas, as most maintain "favorites" lists to circulate among their clients.

Another invaluable tool in easing the photographer selection process is *The Directory for Headshot Photography.* Published annually by Reproductions (whose primary business is reproducing actors' headshots—see the "Headshot Reproduction Services" section in the "Index of Actor Resources and Services"), this free book showcases a wide range of styles and formats by including several examples of the work of each of the city's most sought after photographers. You may pick up a copy of the Directory at Reproductions' office (6 West 37th Street at Fifth Avenue, 4th Floor) or, when available, at The Drama Book Shop (250 West 40th Street, between Seventh and Eighth Avenues). Reproductions also maintains a website which displays most—but not all—of the photographers included in their book. To take a look, go to www.reproductions.com.

Since there are so many headshot photographers out there, trying to see most, if not all, of them is a gargantuan task (and you "Type-A" actors know who you are) that will ultimately be time-consuming and counter productive. Give yourself a break and instead, narrow your search to about eight or so of those who have come recommended or whose work you've seen and liked in the Reproductions directory. Call each and set up an appointment to see their portfolios and to meet with them one-on-one. It is important to schedule time with each not only to discuss the logistics of shooting with them (price, payment policies, style, work methods and session requirements), but also to determine whether or not there is a chemistry and rapport between you. You may love what you see in a portfolio, but if you are not comfortable during the session, or if you don't like the photographer or feel a connection, the final product will reflect those bad feelings.

At the introductory meeting, each photographer will give you a "comp card" (usually an 8 x 10 sheet with several examples of their work), as well as informational material about what you should expect, what to wear, costs, how to prepare for the shoot, how many rolls of film will be shot, the number of prints that come with the session, price for extra prints and/or retouching, a timetable for receiving contact sheets and prints, guarantees or refunds if the prints are unacceptable, etc. Ask questions and take detailed notes of what you're told and what you see in each portfolio; these notes will help in the selection process later. If something in their work stands out, write it down. If you see a pose, composition, or background you like, make note; if you like what someone is wearing in one of the shots, describe it in your notes so that you can go out and find that item or something that approximates it.

Once you've met with all the photographers on your list, seen their work and pored over your notes about each, condense your choices to your three favorites. After you've done this, place the three finalists' comp cards, handouts and your notes in a conspicuous place in your home—a tabletop, dresser, desk, what have you. Each time you see them, ask yourself which "pops" out at you; which does your gut and instincts best react to? Within about a week a clear choice should emerge. Once you've come to a decision, call the photographer you've selected and make your session appointment.

Whatever you do, don't let cost sway your decision. Although I pride myself on living above my means without paying above my means, this is one financial corner I firmly believe should not be cut. View the money you spend on your headshot as a positive investment in your career and future. If your favorite photographer is also the most expensive, for peace of mind and a successful sitting, pay the extra amount. If you go with a photographer solely because of his or her cut rates, you just might get a cut-rate, unusable picture and be out the money you paid for it. A good headshot is too vital to your career to be done on the cheap. If you want to make money in this competitive field, you've got to be willing to spend some, which for a "money shot" will be somewhere between $400 and $1,000.

Preparing for the Session

In the days leading up to the shoot, there are several things you can do to insure the success of both the session and your new headshot:

● Get plenty of rest and try to stay centered and relaxed. Tension and lack of sleep have a way of etching themselves onto a face and are magnified in a black and white photo. Avoid stressful situations and make it your goal to get eight hours of sleep a night. Yoga, meditation and working out are all great tension relievers and contribute to making you look and feel healthy and attractive.

● If you're having your hair cut and/or colored for the shot, do so at least a week before the session to avoid that just cut/colored look.

● Stay out of the sun. Tans and sunburns do not photograph well in a black and white picture.

● For the shoot, you'll want to bring at least eight to twelve changes of clothing. If you need to supplement your wardrobe, give yourself a few days to find and acquire the items that will make you look and feel great. Make sure all clothes you bring to the session are clean and pressed.

● Watch your diet. For the obvious reasons, don't suddenly binge in the days (or hours) before the shoot. Stay away from foods that cause you to break out, keep alcohol consumption to a minimum and drink lots of water.

● All photographers require a deposit of at least half the cost of

the session prior to shooting. Be sure to send the deposit to secure your appointment time. It will be awkward if you arrive
at your appointed time only to find out that it was given to
someone else because you forgot to send in your money. Ask
your photographer about his or her cancellation policy; most
deposits are refundable if you have to cancel and you do it in a
timely manner.

- If you are unsure what you'd like to project in your photo, take
a look at other actors' headshots. You can do this by getting
ahold of *The Directory for Headshot Photography* that I've discussed above, the **Academy Players Directory (APD)** or the
Players' Guide New York (AGNY); the latter two can be found
at the Library for the Performing Arts at Lincoln Center. As I've
said, scrutinizing shots of others will help you pinpoint the
look and essence you'd like to portray.

- If you want to be photographed in glasses, have your op-
tometrist remove the lenses to eliminate glare.

The Shoot

Facing a camera can evoke fear and loathing in the souls of even
the sturdiest, most confident actors. In our work, most of us are
quite comfortable creating the lives of other people, but when it
comes to being ourselves, we balk. Unfortunately, the very nature of the headshot sitting demands that we be nothing but ourselves. Use the following suggestions to help you overcome
tension and any apprehensions you may have developed during the session so that the experience becomes a positive one
yielding an exceptional result:

- Tiredness begets tension, so make it a priority to get eight to ten hours of sleep the night before the big event.

- On the day of the shoot, pamper yourself: eat your favorite foods, listen to your favorite music, do a light workout; if your session is not until the afternoon, don't schedule anything before and make time to squeeze in a nap.

- Allow plenty of time to travel to the studio so that you arrive promptly (and not sweaty) to your appointment.

- Bring your favorite CDs and tapes (otherwise you'll have to put up with the photographer's music) to help you relax and create the mood you'd like to convey in your shot.

- Arrive with the balance due for the session. No photographer I know will shoot you unless you're paid in full. Most only accept cash, certified checks and money orders (for which they'll give you a receipt for tax purposes), so come with the appropriate form of payment. Remember, you will have inquired about payment policies before the session.

- Women should expect the session to last from three to four hours; men should expect two to three hours.

- Men should arrive clean shaven. If you want to do part of your shoot with facial hair, bring shaving accouterments with you.

- Women should seriously consider hiring the photographer's recommended hair and makeup person. Styling for black and white photos requires expertise, so unless you know exactly what you're doing, leave it to the professionals. Moreover, letting someone else take care of your hair and makeup will free you up to relax and focus on the session. Be sure to discuss with the hair and makeup person the image you'd like to project in the photo and the appropriate styling to achieve that image.

● Before facing the camera, make sure that you and your photographer are on the same page regarding the shoot. Discuss in detail all aspects of the session, including lighting (natural vs. artificial), wardrobe, set-ups, indoor/outdoor shots, hair and makeup, as well as what you hope to achieve. If you have an agent or manager, ask what they'd like to see in your photo and give this information to the photographer. Communicate clearly the types of set-ups you want: do you want a **"face"** **shot** (just head and shoulders), **"three quarter" shot** (from about the waist up) or a combination of each. Moreover, do you want the layout to be **"portrait"** style, **"landscape,"** or both?

"Face" Landscape Layout

"Three Quarter" Portrait Layout

● During the shoot, remember that less is more: keep facial expressions small and natural.

● Be spontaneous . . . don't plan or rehearse at home what you're going to do in the studio. Let it happen naturally, organically, and at the prompting of your photographer.

● If you are unsure about what to wear, bring more clothes rather than less. Solid colors and subdued and low-contrast textures such as knits, denim and corduroy photograph well. Clothes that are darker than your skin tone help draw attention to the most important part of the headshot: your face. Bring items that you can layer and several different types of necklines. Wear things that make you feel comfortable, attractive and sexy. Everything should be clean, ironed and in good condition. Men, don't forget to bring a belt and a few different colored tee shirts (white, grey, black) that you can wear alone or layer under other items. Women should bring a selection of bras . . . what works under one outfit may not under another. Avoid clothing that is out of fashion, hyper-trendy or that will upstage you. Likewise, stay away from white and pastels, logos, bulky clothes that hide your body (it's okay to wear things that accentuate your physique as long as they're tasteful and leave something to the imagination), gaudy jewelry, hats, as well as loud prints, patterns and plaids. Above all else, don't dress as a "character." I know an actor who wanted to change his "nice guy" image, so he had headshots made donning "Mafia" attire. His sweet face and demeanor belied his tough guy get-up, rendering his shots ridiculous and a waste of hundreds of dollars. A headshot needs to capture your essence, therefore, wear the kinds of clothes at your session that you wear in your life.

- Yield control of the shoot to your photographer. Take any direction that he or she gives you and trust that they are striving to capture you at your best.

- Be conscious that what your eyes are doing in the shot is essential to its success. In their capacity as "windows to the soul," your eyes, and how much they reveal of your personality and essence, will be what bring the viewer in. Look at any good headshot and you'll see what I mean: you are drawn immediately to the sitter's eyes. Therefore, keep your eyes open, alive, focused and bright. Look directly into the lens (as opposed to away from the lens) but don't stare for too long or they'll begin to freeze up. As I already mentioned, if you want to wear glasses in the shoot, make sure the lenses are removed so that glare does not mask them. And of course, no sunglasses.

- Breathe! When facing a camera we often, without realizing it, hold our breath, making us look stiff, posed and lifeless... the opposite of what we're hoping to achieve.

- There are a couple of relaxation tips, passed on to me by photographers, that help ease the tension created by standing in front of a camera. As well as holding our breath, it is common during a photo session to freeze up and grip muscles, which can also make us look tight (and uptight) and lifeless. The first tip to remedy this is to wiggle your toes. The muscles you use to do this will be in constant motion, keeping the rest of your body from tightening up or becoming static. Secondly, you know that expression, "Make love to the camera"? I don't know what the hell that means really, but try this: Look into the lens as if you are looking at someone you adore and say out loud, "I love you," *in your best Southern accent.* As you do this, warmth, charm, ease and grace will ooze from you. Go ahead, do it now (don't be shy, no one's looking). You see! It works like gangbusters . . . warmth, charm, ease and grace.

• The "lean and hungry" look may be de rigueur for models, but it won't work for you. The session will last a few hours so bring something to snack on as well as water and/or other beverages.

• Turn off your cell phone; receiving calls will be a distraction.

• Don't bring anyone with you to the session; they too will be a distraction.

• Don't drink alcohol or do recreational drugs. Although you may think you need one or the other to help you relax, imbibing either will make you look tired, stupid, or both.

Selecting Your Headshot

About a week after the session, the real fun begins—the headshot selection process. You'll receive a call from your photographer telling you that your contact sheets (pages containing miniature versions of all the shots taken during the session) are ready. Human nature being what it is (curious!), you'll immediately dash over to pick them up. The photographer will have circled his or her favorites and explain why each was chosen. The contact sheets will then be handed to you to take home so that you can choose the shots that will represent you for the next year to several years (depending of course on whether or not your "look" changes drastically in that time).

Go over each meticulously. Try to divorce yourself from the person in the pictures and imagine you are looking at the contact sheets of a stranger. Which shots make you want to know this person? Which pop out at you? Which give you insight into this person? (To assist in viewing the contact sheets, get yourself a photographer's loupe, which magnifies the shots so that you can see details in each. Loupes are cheap and can be found at most photo supply and stationery stores.) Circle, initial or otherwise notate all your choices.

Now it's time to hand them over to everyone in your life: husbands, wives, lovers, friends, colleagues, relatives, teachers, agents, casting people, co-workers, anyone you can corral into looking at them. Ask each their opinions and make note of their responses.

Once you've gotten their choices, go back over each photo. Have you changed your selections based on the opinions of others? Was there a consensus about a particular shot or shots? (There usually is.) Did any or most agree with your choices? A clear favorite may emerge by polling others. Remember, however, that although input from others is welcome and helpful, you must make the final choice. You're going to have to live with the shot for a while and so must select that which you feel best captures you and best says about you what you want it to say.

If the process stymies you or if you feel there are too many good shots to choose from, ask your photographer to print eight-by-tens of the pictures in question (be prepared, though, to pay for any extras beyond those included in the price of the shoot— usually $20 to $30 each). Seeing your choices blown up will help you arrive at a final decision.

When it comes to retouching a print, the opinion in the business of late is that unless there are significant flaws—huge pimples or scars, dark circles around your eyes, or wrinkles deep enough to go rappelling in—don't do it. More and more, the industry wants to see unsullied, natural shots, and few photographers recommend retouching. If you decide to have retouching done, consult with your photographer, as either he or she will do it or refer you to someone who can. As in all headshot "extras," be prepared to pay for retouching.

Reproducing Your Headshot

Once you've received the finished prints from your photographer, it's time to have them reproduced. As this is not a service photographers provide, you'll need to bring them to a lab that does this kind of work. When deciding on which duplication service to go with, ask your photographer for a recommendation, query all the actors you know who they've used and liked, and visit a few labs to find out about prices and services and to see samples of their work. (For a list of several recommended photo reproducers, see "Headshot Reproduction Services" in "Index of Actor Resources and Services.")

When you go to have your shot reproduced, you'll be offered a range of choices as to how you'd like it to appear. You'll be asked the kind of finish and border (if any) you'd prefer and if you wish to include your name on the print.

For finishes, there are a couple to choose from: the **glossy**, which looks slick and, well, glossy, and is reminiscent of the photos that were circulating in the business thirty years ago; and the **matte**, which gives a photo a softer, flatter, less artificial feel, and is currently the more popular of the two.

A border is used much like a picture frame to draw focus to the subject's face. You can go with two styles of borders, or opt for none at all. The **bottom border** is a white band that appears below the picture and is usually used to display the actor's name:

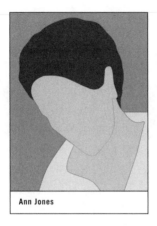

Ann Jones

The **full border** (the more popular of the two) is a white inch-thick frame that is round the print on all four sides:

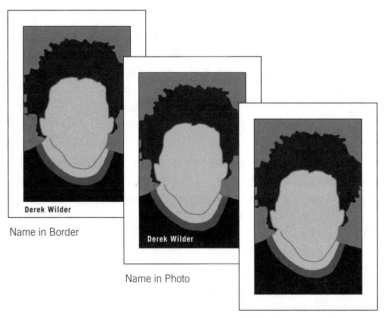

Derek Wilder

Name in Border

Derek Wilder

Name in Photo

No Name

You can also opt for no border at all:

Name in Photo   No Name

For those starting out in the business, you should include your name on the lower part of your print. Printing your name in black on a white border will help make it stand out; if you choose to put your name on the photo itself, use white lettering to give it prominence. Once you're established and people in the biz get to know you, it's up to you whether or not you want to include your name.

When ordering your initial set of prints, I suggest getting between one and two hundred. Unlike the acting rule "less is more," the opposite is true for headshots: the more you order, the less you'll pay per shot. For example, most labs charge almost $100 for fifty reproductions (almost $2 a shot). Whereas 100 go for around $120 (about $1.20 a shot), 200 are approximately $190 (less than $1 per picture) and 500 are about $350 (about 70¢ per shot). You will be sending lots of pictures out in pursuit of agent representation, auditions and work, so it'll be cost effective to have more of these in hand than less. (Be aware that the cost of sending out your headshot adds up: you'll also need to buy envelopes, stationery for cover letters, and postage.)

As an alternative to photo-reproduced headshots, a few labs offer lithographed prints. The difference in price is tremendous, with the litho prints costing almost twenty-five percent less. There was a time when the litho was spurned because it looked shoddy and wasn't nearly as sharp as its counterpart. Today, duplication technology has advanced to such a degree that there is almost no discernible difference between the two. For a great product and a lower price tag, it's a no-brainer...go with lithographs. (Note: If you have agent representation, be sure to ask how she or he feels about lithos; industry opinion about this process is split right down the middle—some agents like them, some don't. The most common complaint is that they are not quite as sharp as regular photos and, because they are printed on thick paper stock, they are difficult to fax.)

When you pick up your reproduced photos, ask the lab if they will keep a copy of your headshot on file. Most offer this service to expedite the ordering process—with your headshot on file, whenever you need a new batch printed up, you can call and place your order over the phone.

The desired outcome of a reproduced print is that it looks just like the original. If it doesn't, explain your qualms to the lab. You should not send out a badly reproduced shot, as it will surely be tossed in the trash upon receipt, leave a bad impression about you in the industry, as well as be a waste of your hard-earned money. If the lab can't—or won't—rectify the problem, demand a refund and go elsewhere. Most labs do strive to please their customers (hoping you'll be back many times) and will work with you until you are satisfied.

Resumes

Stiff Competition, Part 2

The way you present yourself on your resume is as vital to your acting career as a great headshot. Your resume lets the industry know what you've done and can do, where you've studied, and the skills you possess. It not only promotes you to the powers that be, it also demonstrates to them that you take your craft seriously and have the requisite experience, training and skills for any role you're cast in. Hopefully, they'll see something on your resume that sparks their interest and entices them to bring you in for an audition or meeting.

I've said it before and I'll say it again: the competition in our business is fierce. So, the more you know about creating a good resume, the better your chances are of getting inside the offices of agents and casting directors.

Creating an Attention-Getting Resume

The best resume is simple, straightforward, and legible. It must be typewritten in black ink, proofread for typos and misspellings, and printed on a single sheet of plain white or off-white paper (the quality of paper doesn't matter). The paper should be exactly eight by ten inches, the same size as your headshot, and stapled to your photo on all four corners. For a more varied and eye-catching appearance, use a couple of different fonts and type sizes and styles; however, avoid fonts that are too "cute" or illegible. Unlike a resume you'd need for a job in the real world, your acting resume should only include information that is directly related to your career. Although you may have a Ph.D. in nuclear medicine, served in the Peace Corps, or invented the internet, the industry doesn't care—it just wants to know that you can act. The contents of your resume should be neatly organized into four categories:

1. Heading and Contact Information

The "Heading" at the top of your resume contains, among other things, your name written in large, bold letters. Below or next to your name, list your union affiliations, if any. Most importantly, the heading should contain your correct, up-to-date contact information. If an agent or casting person likes what he or she sees and wants to bring you in but can't or doesn't know how to reach you, you lose. (Note: As you won't always know who will end up with your resume and headshot, never list your home phone number or address; instead, use a cell, beeper, pager or answering service number, e-mail address and web address if you have one. If you already have agent representation, include their name, logo, and contact information in lieu of your own.) The heading should include your statistics: height, eye and hair color, and, if you sing, your vocal range (tenor, alto, etc.). While some actors include their weight on their resumes, others believe that that information, like age, is no one's business but their own; it's your call as to whether or not you want to include it.

"Heading" examples:

MEREDITH PORTER
AEA, AFTRA, SAG

Height:	5'3"	212-555-0000
Weight:	107	mpter@porterhouse.com
Hair:	Red	www.porterhouse.com

Fanny Crumble

917-555-2222 / fanny@blabla.com

Height:	5'5"
Hair:	Brunette
Eyes:	Brown
Voice:	Alto

---

909 Seventh Avenue, New York, NY 10019
212-555-8888
TOM'S NIFTY TALENT AGENCY

TNT

Martin Green   AEA—SAG—AFTRA

Hair: Brown / Eyes: Brown / Height: 5'4" / Voice: Countertenor

---

2. Experience

The "Experience" section should take up the bulk of your resume. Here you will *truthfully* list your acting credits, divided into
three main sections: "New York Theater," "Film and Television,"
and "Regional Theater." List first either the most impressive credits, or your experiences in the area of the business you most want
to pursue (e.g., if your primary goal is to work in film and television, list those credits first).

With your TV and film credits, include the name of the project, the role you played, the type of role or "billing" (e.g. "recurring"—a character that is featured on a few episodes of a regular show; "lead" or "star"—the starring role; "co-star," "guest star," "principal" or "featured"—a large role on a show that is not the lead; "day-player"—a principal role played by a guest actor for one to several days in a film, soap or TV show; "under-five"—an actor in a soap who has five lines or less of dialogue), and the director and production company:

Law and Order	Tammy Hines (co-star)	NBC/Joe Golden

The More the Merrier	Mary Morton (lead)	Columbia/Mickey Mann

All My Children	Brick Hurtwell (day-player)	ABC/Bill Smith

For theater credits, list the play, your character, the theater and director:

The Skin of Our Teeth	Sabina	Roundabout Theater Co./Bill Espy

Including directors and producers or theater companies is beneficial, because an industry person may see on your resume the name of a reputable organization or someone whom he or she knows or whose work they respect, and will bring you in solely because of your affiliation. Remember, our business is tiny and everyone knows (or has heard of) everyone else.

In the "Experience" section, you may also want to list other work such as industrials, stand-up comedy, cabaret performances, internet appearances, and so on. Never list individual commercials, however. Since most run for only one or two cycles (usually thirteen weeks per cycle), by including commercial credits on your resume, you could ostensibly be keeping yourself from getting more of this kind of work. (If, for example, you did a McDonald's commercial two years ago but it is no longer airing, and casting directors for Burger King see that credit on your resume, they may think the spot is still running and refrain from bringing you in on their project.) For commercial listings on your resume, it's best to say, "List available upon request."

Extra work should not be included, either. Industry folk have an uncanny way of sussing out background work from actual roles on a resume, and being an extra is not acting.

3. Training

After the "Experience" section, you should list all of the acting and performance related classes you've taken, the people you've trained under, and the workshops, seminars, programs or institutions you've attended. Include your college or grad school degree if it is acting related. Industry people are particularly interested in actors' educational backgrounds, especially those just starting out who don't yet have a lot of professional credits. When trying to determine whether or not you have "the goods," the "Training" section of your resume will give them a pretty clear idea.

"Training" examples:

"Camera Basics"—Richard Forrester—New York Acting Academy

M.F.A. in Acting—Yale School of Drama, class of 2000

"Shakespeare and His Contemporaries"—Will Kemp—Shakespeare Institute

Voice: Vinnie Moskowitz (7 years)

Dance: Ballet (8 years), Jazz (3 years)—Steps, New York

4. Special Skills

If you have any skills at which you are *extremely proficient*, list them at the bottom of your resume. Special skills can include anything from dancing and singing, to foreign languages, dialects, stage combat, sports, hobbies, unusual talents, and musical instruments you play. Catalog anything that might set you apart from the competition; skills or abilities you possess that others don't may be exactly the things that help you land a job.

For example:

Special Skills: Spanish native speaker, dialects (all British, American Southern, Russian, French, German), dance (merengue, cumbia and jazz), lighting and sound equipment experience, driver license, yodel, scuba diver (certified), expert skier, piano and guitar, can knot a cherry stem with my tongue

A word to the wise: don't claim you're an expert at a skill unless you truly are. If you are cast in a film or commercial because your resume said you are a "Black Diamond" skier, but you can't even snowplow down the bunny slope, you'll be fired from the job, blacklisted by the production company and become *persona non grata* for the rest of your life with the casting director.

What to Do If You Have Little or No Professional Experience

Not too long ago, a young actress I know who had only been in the business a short time began freelancing with an agent at one of the city's mid-size offices. During a visit one afternoon, the agent asked my friend if she'd like to meet a woman who had just joined the agency as a talent representative. The actress of course said yes and was ushered into the new agent's office. What my friend didn't know was that this new agent, an elderly woman who had previously been a commercial casting director for decades, is well known in the business for being unkind, ungracious and tactless.

The meeting was a disaster: The agent asked the actress to do a monologue, cutting her off midway through with, "Stop, stop, stop. You're not at all right for this role." The agent then glanced at the actress's headshot and blurted, "You look like a slut in this picture." Adding a final insult, she turned the headshot over, perused the resume for a moment, then threw her hands up to shade her eyes and exclaimed melodramatically, "My god, I need sunglasses! I'm being blinded by the reflection coming off of all the blank space on this resume." Being the first time the young actress had experienced this kind of abuse, she was reduced to tears.

Don't let this extreme example of bad behavior by one unpleasant woman daunt you. Ninety-nine point nine percent of the business understands the dilemma of the novice actor who is either fresh out of school or who has little or no professional experience. It is a classic Catch-22 situation: with few or no credits, it's hard to get seen for roles, yet you need those roles to build your resume. There are ways in which you can pad your resume, however, in order to avoid an episode like this.

Start by utilizing the trick we all learned the first time we had to write a college term paper: use large fonts to fill up the page and double-space between categories.

Next, fill out your resume by listing each and every performance-related class you've taken, including dance, voice, speech, Alexander technique, etc. The same can be said for your "Special Skills" section; include *anything* that is or can be construed as a skill...as long as you are proficient at it.

Finally, include any—and I mean *any*—acting experience you may have had. Did you play the camel in Sister Immaculata's high school Christmas pageant? Include that. Just don't say it was high school, and don't say it was a camel. (Give your camel character a name instead, something like "Camille.") You spoke one line in a student film that has no hope of being seen, even by the director's family? Give that character a name and say it was a "lead" (after all, if no one's going to see it, who's going to know?).

What's that you say? It sounds like I am telling you to fudge the truth? Although some disagree, many believe that in the beginning of your career, you should, dare I say it, LIE! But, the lies should be small, insignificant lies, no more than minor fibs—little white lies that are impossible to refute. Here's how...

If you did any acting in high school or college, put those plays and roles down (the same applies to characters you have worked on extensively in an acting class), but don't say they were academic credits. Instead, make up a theater, perhaps incorporating the name of your hometown ("*Poughkeepsie* Little Players") or your mother's maiden name ("*Smith* Theatre Collaborative").

Having said that, if you are going to fib, make sure you know

y and part you're lying about inside and out. Also, dis-
in a way in which you cannot get caught. Don't use the
of real people or existing theaters. If during a meeting or
on you are asked about a particular listing ("I'm from
keepsie and I didn't know there was a community theater
."), have a reply ready, something along the lines of, "Oh,
hat theater burned down five years ago." Or, "It recently
e a 7-Eleven." Again, whatever you do, don't claim you
d at a theater that really exists, or with an actual director.
said, everyone knows everyone in this business (and they
e steel-trap memories to boot) and you will be caught.
alienate the person who catches you in the lie and proba-
n't be given a chance to redress your wrongs. (A director
tells this story: "I was once auditioning a woman and was
sed to see she had the name of a certain director on her re-
After her audition, I asked her how she liked working with
s Morey, the director she had included. 'Oh, it was a great
ence,' she replied. 'He's a wonderful guy and a wonderful
or.' I thanked the actress for coming in and said goodbye.
was walking out the door, I said, 'By the way, I've never
es on you before in my life, and I'm Charles Morey.' " Do
to tell you that she was never brought in to audition for
gain?)
at the industry doesn't know about (nor do they care to
about for that matter) is every little, out-of-the-way, non-
sional or community theater you've worked in. All they
to know is if you've had any experience in front of an audi-
if you can say your lines without bumping into the furni-
nd if you can create a character. Minor fibs such as these
nem some assurance that you have, you won't and you can.
in mind, however, that if you've got any white lies on your
e, your number one priority will be to purge those (by land-
gitimate acting work) as quickly as you can.

M.F.A. in Acting—Yale School of Drama, class of 2000

"Shakespeare and His Contemporaries"—Will Kemp—Shakespeare Institute

Voice: Vinnie Moskowitz (7 years)

Dance: Ballet (8 years), Jazz (3 years)—Steps, New York

4. Special Skills

If you have any skills at which you are *extremely proficient*, list them at the bottom of your resume. Special skills can include anything from dancing and singing, to foreign languages, dialects, stage combat, sports, hobbies, unusual talents, and musical instruments you play. Catalog anything that might set you apart from the competition; skills or abilities you possess that others don't may be exactly the things that help you land a job.

For example:

Special Skills: Spanish native speaker, dialects (all British, American Southern, Russian, French, German), dance (merengue, cumbia and jazz), lighting and sound equipment experience, driver license, yodel, scuba diver (certified), expert skier, piano and guitar, can knot a cherry stem with my tongue

A word to the wise: don't claim you're an expert at a skill unless you truly are. If you are cast in a film or commercial because your resume said you are a "Black Diamond" skier, but you can't even snowplow down the bunny slope, you'll be fired from the job, blacklisted by the production company and become *persona non grata* for the rest of your life with the casting director.

the play and part you're lying about inside and out. Also, dissemble in a way in which you cannot get caught. Don't use the names of real people or existing theaters. If during a meeting or audition you are asked about a particular listing ("I'm from Poughkeepsie and I didn't know there was a community theater there . . ."), have a reply ready, something along the lines of, "Oh, geez, that theater burned down five years ago." Or, "It recently became a 7-Eleven." Again, whatever you do, don't claim you worked at a theater that really exists, or with an actual director. As I've said, everyone knows everyone in this business (and they all have steel-trap memories to boot) and you will be caught. You'll alienate the person who catches you in the lie and probably won't be given a chance to redress your wrongs. (A director friend tells this story: "I was once auditioning a woman and was surprised to see she had the name of a certain director on her resume. After her audition, I asked her how she liked working with Charles Morey, the director she had included. 'Oh, it was a great experience,' she replied. 'He's a wonderful guy and a wonderful director.' I thanked the actress for coming in and said goodbye. As she was walking out the door, I said, 'By the way, I've never laid eyes on you before in my life, and I'm Charles Morey.' " Do I need to tell you that she was never brought in to audition for him again?)

What the industry doesn't know about (nor do they care to know about for that matter) is every little, out-of-the-way, nonprofessional or community theater you've worked in. All they want to know is if you've had any experience in front of an audience, if you can say your lines without bumping into the furniture, and if you can create a character. Minor fibs such as these give them some assurance that you have, you won't and you can. Keep in mind, however, that if you've got any white lies on your resume, your number one priority will be to purge those (by landing legitimate acting work) as quickly as you can.

What to Do If You Have Little or No Professional Experience

Not too long ago, a young actress I know who had only been in the business a short time began freelancing with an agent at one of the city's mid-size offices. During a visit one afternoon, the agent asked my friend if she'd like to meet a woman who had just joined the agency as a talent representative. The actress of course said yes and was ushered into the new agent's office. What my friend didn't know was that this new agent, an elderly woman who had previously been a commercial casting director for decades, is well known in the business for being unkind, ungracious and tactless.

The meeting was a disaster: The agent asked the actress to do a monologue, cutting her off midway through with, "Stop, stop, stop. You're not at all right for this role." The agent then glanced at the actress's headshot and blurted, "You look like a slut in this picture." Adding a final insult, she turned the headshot over, perused the resume for a moment, then threw her hands up to shade her eyes and exclaimed melodramatically, "My god, I need sunglasses! I'm being blinded by the reflection coming off of all the blank space on this resume." Being the first time the young actress had experienced this kind of abuse, she was reduced to tears.

Don't let this extreme example of bad behavior by one unpleasant woman daunt you. Ninety-nine point nine percent of the business understands the dilemma of the novice actor who is either fresh out of school or who has little or no professional experience. It is a classic Catch-22 situation: with few or no credits, it's hard to get seen for roles, yet you need those roles to build

your resume. There are ways in which you ca[n] however, in order to avoid an episode like th[is]

Start by utilizing the trick we all learned t[he] to write a college term paper: use large font[s] and double-space between categories.

Next, fill out your resume by listing performance-related class you've taken, incl[uding] speech, Alexander technique, etc. The same [in the] "Special Skills" section; include *anything* th[at can be con-] strued as a skill . . . as long as you are proficie[nt].

Finally, include any—and I mean *any*—ac[ting] may have had. Did you play the camel in [your] high school Christmas pageant? Include th[at. If it] was high school, and don't say it was a cam[el, give the] character a name instead, something like "C[. . .] one line in a student film that has no hope o[f . . .] the director's family? Give that character a [. . .] a "lead" (after all, if no one's going to se[e it, who will] know?).

What's that you say? It sounds like I am [. . .] the truth? Although some disagree, many b[elieve at the be-] ginning of your career, you should, dare I [say it, lie. The] lies should be small, insignificant lies, no m[ore than] little white lies that are impossible to refut[e].

If you did any acting in high school or co[llege, put those shows] and roles down (the same applies to c[haracters you] worked on extensively in an acting class[, even if they] were academic credits. Instead, make up [a theater, in-] corporating the name of your hometown [(i.e., "Centerville] Players") or your mother's maiden name [(i.e., "The Smith Col-] laborative").

Having said that, if you are going to fib,

Sample Resume

Alex Martin

AEA – AFTRA – SAG

Hair: Blond	212-555-3456	Height: 5'11"
Eyes: Grey	alexmar@blabla.com	Voice: Baritone

NEW YORK THEATER

Coconuts (Broadway)	Kenny (understudy)	Cort Theater/Sara Fine
Girl's Life	Tim	Strasberg Theater/Adam Russell
As You Like It	Orlando	Classic Co./Corey Naperstein
Angels in America	Prior Walter	LAB Theatre/Diana Dew
The Lion in Winter	Prince Richard	Studio Players/Amanda Kelly

FILM & TELEVISION

The Last 200 Years	Karl Brech (principal)	Disney Films/Bret Brown
Law and Order	Frat Boy (featured)	NBC/Dick Wolfe
Law and Order: S.V.U.	Milton Fromer (co-star)	NBC/Ted Gotcha
The Lottery Ticket	Andy (principal)	Ind. Feature/Carl Tucci
One Life to Live	Hoodlum #2 (under-five)	ABC
Spying Game	Dark Raider (principal)	NYU Student Film/Kramer Latchkey

REGIONAL

Hamlet	Hamlet	Guthrie Theatre/Dennis Washington
Arcadia	Septimus	Seattle Repertory Theatre/David Strong
Beyond Therapy	Bob	Long Wharf Theatre/Arvin Black
True West	Austin	Berkeley Rep./Sam Spiritu
The Dining Room	Actor Three	New Jersey Shakespeare/Mike Tello
Henry V	Chorus	Shakespeare Theatre/Miguel Moran

INDUSTRIAL

Interactive E-Learning Training Video	Lawyer	Diversity Films/Connie Banks
United Nations Presentation	Teacher	OneWorld Prods./Josh Stram
Living Will	Host	Med. Educ. Svcs./Rowan Twomey
Moving Ahead	Student	Berlitz Industrials/Jon Halley

Voice-over (demo available upon request)

Commercials (list and conflicts available upon request)

TRAINING

Acting—M.F.A. in Acting, University of Delaware, Newark, DE
Steppenwolf Theatre Co. Summer Program—Kurt Columbus, Beverly Grobin
"On Camera"—Brian Harwood—New York Acting Academy
Improv—Geoffrey Milton, Julie Montagu, Tommy Hendrix
Commercials—Sally Levi, Jack Johnson, Leroy Daley
Stage Combat—Mordechai Knott, Orlando Ferguson
Voice—Joyce Ariel (singing), Jackie Farr (speech)

SPECIAL SKILLS: Saxophone, certified in stage combat (all), French fluent, ice skate, juggle, rollerblade, ski (expert), dialects (all British and American, French, German, Italian)

Updating Your Resume

As your experience expands and your career flourishes, you'll want your resume to reflect each new job, class or acquired skill. Just as you would update your headshot if the way you look has changed, so too should you revise your resume with each new role. With the proliferation of personal computers, it is no longer difficult or time-consuming to create and maintain your own resume. Corrections to your resume can be quickly inserted, although one or two minor handwritten changes or additions are acceptable; any more than that and it will look messy.

If you don't trust your resume-creating abilities or are hopeless with a computer, there are a couple of companies that will do it for you at a price. (See the "Resume Services" section of the "Index of Actor Resources and Services.") These services will not only tailor and print a handsome, personalized, professional resume for you, they will also store it in their database so that with a simple phone call, they can update it for you whenever you need it. Charges range from $150 to $165 for creating a resume and printing fifty copies. Changes cost anywhere from $7 to a whopping $32.50 (which includes fifty copies of your resume).

Resume Checklist

☑ Type your resume in black ink and print it on a single sheet of white or off-white paper.

☑ Proofread the resume for typos and misspelled words; mistakes will reflect badly on you.

☑ Your resume should be 8 x 10 so that it fits neatly against the back of your headshot.

☑ Use a couple of font sizes, types and styles for a more captivating appearance; avoid "cute" or illegible fonts.

☑ Include only information that is pertinent to your acting career.

☑ Organize your resume tidily into four categories:

  ☑ Heading—displays your name prominently, your current contact information (do not use your home telephone number or address), union affiliations, agent representation and statistics (height, weight, hair and eye color and vocal range … do not list your age).

  ☑ Experience—lists your acting credits, beginning with the most prominent or important roles. Categorize these entries into three general areas: "New York Theater," "Film and Television," and "Regional." From left to right, list the name of the project, the role you played (if it's a film or TV role, tell what type of role it was—"recurring," "co-star," "day-player," etc.), the theater or production company, and the director. Use subheadings to list other acting work such as industrials, voice-overs, student films, stand-up comedy. Under "Commercials" do not itemize the commercials you have done; instead, write "List available upon request."

  ☑ Training—lists all acting-related classes, seminars, workshops, institutions you've attended, and the teachers and coaches you've studied with.

  ☑ Special Skills—includes all unique or unusual abilities you possess that will help you stand out from the crowd; don't claim you are proficient at something unless you really are.

☑ Staple your resume to all four corners of your headshot.

☑ Update your resume with each new role, class or acquired skill. If your contact information changes, make sure your resume reflects those changes.

Mailings and Marketing

The Mailing

You've got the headshot. You've got the resume. Now it's time to place them into the hands of potential employers or those who may help you find work.

Succeeding in this business requires your proactive participation in marketing yourself to the powers that be. A "mailing" is just the thing to help you achieve that end. Basically, a mailing is any correspondence by actors for the purpose of introducing themselves to, or communicating with, people in "the business." It is probably the most powerful way for an actor to promote himself/herself to directors, casting directors, producers and agents. Most of these industry people, who have the muscle to employ us, hate being cold called or visited unexpectedly, making it challenging (to say the least) to connect with them. A mailing provides a non-intrusive and professional avenue for presenting yourself, keeping in touch, and informing these powers that be when you are working.

The objective of a mailing is to promote yourself in such a way that you capture their attention in the hope of securing an audition, interview or job. A mailing also gives the industry an opportunity to see sides of you that are not evident in a picture or resume: your personality, creativity and professionalism.

Though there are several kinds of mailings (discussed below), some general rules apply to each:

- Use a simple white or manila colored envelope; for the correspondence part of your mailing, you may use fine grade/bond paper, but plain white is perfectly acceptable.

- Always address your mailing to specific individuals and make sure their names are spelled correctly—misspelling an agent's or casting director's name or addressing your message to "Sir," "Madam," or "Whom It May Concern" will leave a bad impression. Likewise, know the sex of the person to whom you are writing. Unsure if Toby is a Mr. or Adrian a Ms.? Then call their office and ask.

- All correspondence coming from you should have your current contact information and union affiliations.

- Unless your handwriting is legible, handprint, type or word-process and print out all correspondence (if you handwrite a letter, use blue or black ink). If you are helpless at computer skills, consider having a professional do your mailings for you. (For the companies that do this kind of work, see "Resume Services" in "Index of Actor Resources and Services.")

- Your communication should be concise (no more than a few sentences), as well as personal, affable, informative, professional, charismatic and engaging. The industry receives hundreds of these each day; those that are original, upbeat and show that you both understand how the business works and that you take it seriously are going to garner their notice.

- In your cover letter, state the purpose of your correspondence: what you want and why you're writing.

- Talk about your career achievements, objectives and expectations.

- Don't be pushy, demanding or sound psychotic (unless it's your desire to sabotage your career).

- Check for typos and misspellings.

- Personally sign all correspondence.

- Keep a record of all those you send your mailings to, and when you send them. Knowing how often you write, and to whom, will, hopefully, keep you from inundating offices with too many mailings too often. Limit your contact to no more than once a month.

- Most importantly, always have a reason for contacting industry people. Sending a "Just wanted to keep in touch" note with no new information or specific end takes up an agent's or casting director's limited time and creates resentment... the last thing you want is anyone in the industry resenting you.

- Be sure to put the correct postage on all mailings.

Types of Mailings

The types of mailings that best benefit actors include:

1. The Contact Mailing

The "contact" mailing is an actor's means of communicating with both talent agents when seeking representation and casting people to inquire about auditions. In the contact mailing, you will want to include with your cover letter a picture and resume, demo reel (a VHS or DVD copy of the best moments of an actor's work on film, television and commercials; it is used to

Sample Contact Cover Letter:

Sally Blakely
799 West 44th Street, Apt. 74-G, New York, NY 10000
212-555-0088

Tom Morgan
c/o The Morgan Agency
1 Sixth Avenue, Suite 9999
New York, NY 10055

Dear Mr. Morgan:

My name is Sally, and I have just arrived in NYC after graduating from UNC with a B.A. in Drama. I have had a lot of on camera training, have worked on various industrials and independent films and am very comfortable in front of a camera.

At this point in my career, I'm particularly interested in doing commercials (I just shot a national network spot for Sprint, which I landed without an agent). I am writing you in hopes of scheduling a meeting to discuss working together. My mother Rose Blakely (your godmother) thought we'd collaborate well!

If you are interested in meeting, I may be reached at 212-555-0088.

Thanks so much, and I hope to hear from you.

Sincerely,

Sally Blakely

market talent, type and range to anyone who can help actors get work—for more information on demos, see the chapter "Demo Reels and Working on Film") or voice-over reel, and any other promotional materials, like reviews of your work, any articles that have been written about you or other kinds of publicity that will assist in "selling" you to the person you are writing to.

The body of your letter should include your name, up-to-date contact information, union affiliations (if any), and any personal connection you may have to the addressee ("Your brother Bob is my best friend and he suggested I write you," "Your client Corey Blotnik has urged me to send you my picture and resume"). Give a brief description of your experience (include only a few of the most recent or notable projects) and training. State the purpose of the mailing . . . that you are requesting an interview or audition. If you are contacting an agent, include the names of some of the casting directors whom you know or have met; this will give them an idea of how far along you are on your career path. Always know the expertise of the people you are contacting and target them accordingly. You don't want to write to a commercial agent if you are seeking "legit" representation; a Broadway casting director probably can't help you if you want to do voice-overs.

2. The Invitation Mailing

When doing a play, showcase, reading or workshop in the city, you may want to invite industry people to see you perform. For this kind of mailing, include enticements like informational or press materials about the project and reviews (if favorable, of course). Also, if available, offer complimentary tickets. Know, however, that you probably won't hear from many (or any) agents or casting directors, unless of course you are in a bona fide hit. Instead, view the "invitation" mailing as a promotional opportunity to once again get your name and face in front of industry folk and let them know what you are up to.

3. The Thank You Mailing

To keep yourself fresh in the minds of agents or casting directors whom you've recently met with or auditioned for, consider sending a "Thank You" or "I enjoyed meeting you" note. Certainly send a thank you to anyone who has helped you obtain work. This will display to the industry that you are appreciative and have good manners; they will no doubt remember your graciousness the next time they are working on a project that you are right for. When thanking agents or casting directors for meeting you, remind them when you met, what you discussed and ask them to keep you in mind for future projects. For this kind of mailing, you may use either regular notepaper and matching envelope or a Hallmark type Thank You greeting card. Like all other mailings, keep your Thank You notes short and sweet. Moreover, be selective about the frequency with which you send these . . . too many will come off as nothing more than nagging ploys to remind the industry of your existence.

4. The Press Mailing

The best reason for contacting people in "the business" is to let them know when you are working. You'll hear over and over, "Let me know when you're in something." So, do!

The "press" mailing may include everything from a notice of current or future work, to snippets of favorable reviews, acting related news, or achievements such as callbacks, first refusals, completed classes or acquired skills. The press mailing should always be newsworthy and, as in all other types of mailings, brief. To create a compelling press mailing, use various sizes, colors and styles of fonts, as well as pictures (your headshot, a production shot from a play, film or TV show you've appeared in, etc.) and graphics.

Press Mailing Samples:

OLIVIA ROBINSON

is keeping very busy:

She recently closed in the hit Broadway production of *John's Ashes*, directed by Ken Cormack.

This week she can be seen TWICE on TV:

Third Watch
(Co-Star—Airs April 14, 10 P.M. Monday, NBC)
&
Guiding Light
(Day Player: Nurse Nancy—
Air Dates: 4/16 & 4/18, 10 A.M., Monday, CBS)

Conrad/Meyers Talent Reps.
4321 Eighth Avenue, Suite 47, New York, NY 10019
212-555-0000

5. The Picture Postcard Mailing

Picture postcards, which are a miniature version of your head-shot, are probably the best, most economical way to keep in touch with "the business." They are cheaper to send than a letter or 8 x 10

RANDY COOPER

is currently playing Brutus in the acclaimed production of

Julius Caesar

at the Manhattan Actor's Collective

Here's what the critics had to say:

"Not since Olivier have I seen a finer stage actor. Randy Cooper is a force to be reckoned with." —Megan Porter, *NYC Gazette*

"Randy Cooper plays to perfection Brutus' torment and guilt . . . his death scene is worth the price of admission." —Susan McAllen, *Gotham News*

"'Brilliant' is such a hackneyed word, but it's the only thing that comes to mind in trying to describe Mr. Cooper's remarkable portrayal of Brutus. This is a performance you'll be telling your grandkids about." —Scott Bowles, *The Daily & Weekly*

"This guy Cooper is one badass actor." —Celia Bennett, *Vocal Village*

For complimentary tickets, please contact me at: 646-555-6666

and less costly to reproduce than a headshot (order postcards from the same lab that reproduced your photo). Agents and casting people appreciate receiving postcards for their convenience; instead of having to open an envelope and pull out a headshot, the postcard

presents your picture on one side and correspondence on the other. Moreover, as space on a postcard is limited, you won't, to the industry's relief, have room to write your life story.

A postcard is not only the best way to keep in touch with those in the industry whom you have met or auditioned for, it is an ideal means of sending Thank You notes or press mailings. You will definitely want to send a postcard as a follow-up to those to whom you sent a contact mailing. (Note: To avoid hitting them too frequently with mailings, wait at least one month before following up with a postcard.) To insure that the person you are writing to knows exactly who you are, have your correct contact information and union affiliations printed on the same side of the postcard as your photo.

Although postcards are easy and cheap to send, don't overdo it. Always have a specific purpose for sending a postcard and, as I said above, don't mail to the same person more than once a month.

Examples of postcard mailings
(both sides):

AEA   **Paul Goodwin**   AFTRA
212-555-6789

Hi, Sandra:

You can catch me on *Law & Order* this Wednesday at 10 P.M. (NBC). I'm playing the murderer *du jour!* Also, I was just placed on First Refusal for a national American Express spot.

Best,

Paul

Sandra Daley
SD Casting Associates
444 Ninth Avenue
Room 908
New York, NY 10039

Hi, Mr. Pietrantone:

It was great meeting you this week—and thanks for the kind feedback about my monologue. I'm pleased that you want to work with me (I'll drop off the 40 pics and resumes you requested by the end of the week) and I look forward to getting started.

Sincerely,

Olivia

Tom Pietrantone
A-One Talent
908 West 53rd Street
Suite 111
New York, NY 10099

Hi, Julia:

I hear you're about to cast *The Deep End* for Miramax and are looking for actors who swim. Don't know if you're aware, but before I was an actor, I was an Olympic swimmer (no medals, alas!). I'd love to read for you.

Warmly,

Ron

Julia Verner
Enigma Casting Assocs.
12345 Third Avenue
Suite 678
New York, NY 10080

Your Mailing List

To run your acting corporation efficiently, you'll want to maintain an accurate list of business contacts. These are the people you will be sending mailings to, whose names can be kept on computer disk or database, Rolodex, printed list, labels, index cards, or any other system that you prefer. Your mailing list should comprise two categories:

1. The industry people you have met, know or auditioned for

2. Those you want to meet, know, and audition for

This way you can gear your mailings accordingly. As you become familiar with those in the second category, move their names and contact information to the first.

Make sure you've got the correct contact and office information for each person on your mailing list. To improve the rate of success of your mailings, update your records monthly. The powers that be in our business are constantly moving from one office to another, advancing to other positions, or getting out of the business altogether. For up-to-the-minute information on agents, casting directors and producers, consult the *Ross Reports*, considered the best source to go to when compiling data for your mailing lists. (For a detailed description, see the "Periodicals and Theater Related Publications" section of the "Index of Actor Resources and Services.")

Can't be bothered creating your own lists? A handful of companies have done the work for you by creating myriad types of affordable (between $8 and $20), updated mailing list labels so that you can reach anyone in the business you choose. These labels can be found at most stores specializing in drama books or through their websites (refer to the "Mailing Labels" and "Bookstores" sections of the "Index of Actor Resources and Services").

Following Up

Although some teachers and business coaches advocate following up a mailing with a phone call or visit, I say do it at your own peril. The many business people I know and have spoken to agree: contacting them via a mailing does not give you carte blanche to hound them with calls or drop-ins. When marketing yourself to the industry, your aim should be to present yourself in as positive a way as possible. All your hard work (not to mention the cash you've spent to market yourself) will be for naught if you alienate agents and casting directors and their secretaries by calling or dropping by unannounced. Don't do it. If these people are interested in meeting or auditioning you, they will be in contact. Only call if you've been asked to call; only drop by if you have a scheduled appointment.

The most effective and professional way to follow up a mailing is with another mailing. Send a postcard, Thank You note, or press mailing. Remind those you are writing to of previous correspondence, meetings or auditions, and restate your reason for contacting them (e.g., "I sent my picture and resume to you about four months ago and am following up to see if you've had a chance to look them over. I'm still very interested in meeting you and discussing the possibility of working together. Since writing you last, I've done the following... ").

Even though you will expend a lot of time, energy and money on your mailings, expect the rate of response to be low in the beginning. Very few agents and casting directors have the time to go through every piece of mail they receive. If only a fraction of the city's 90,000 actors sent mailings, that would still be an enormous amount of invitations, Thank You notes, fliers, headshots and resumes, postcards, review packets and exhortations for auditions and interviews to go through. To stand out from the crowd, you will have to do your mailings with some frequency and persistence. (Note: Don't be like the many actors who, when they don't realize their desired results after the first round, forego doing mailings ever again.)

Let the industry know what you're doing and what you've done on a regular basis. By continually seeing your name, head-shot and mailings before them, agents and casting directors will eventually take notice. Diligence, patience and stick-to-itiveness (along with creativity and an upbeat attitude) will pay off. The in-dustry likes to work with "winners" and periodically keeping them abreast of your successes and achievements will help woo them into wanting to work with you.

Other Ways to Market Yourself

Besides mailings, there are a few other marketing tools you can utilize to successfully "sell" yourself to the industry. These in-clude:

Photo business cards . . . Carried conveniently in your wallet or pocket, these come in handy during chance meetings with agents or casting directors (or anyone else for that matter). If someone asks how to reach you and you don't have a picture and resume, hand them one of your cards. (They should be the same size as a regular business card and display your picture and contact phone number.) Most photo reproduction labs offer this service at a rel-atively inexpensive price (about $80 for 150 business cards to $195 for 1000); if you own a computer and printer, you can create them yourself.

Actor directories . . . There are two leading performer directories in which you may list yourself for a fee. Both are respected and used by a lot of industry people:

Established in 1937, the *Academy Players Directory (APD)* is the first and oldest publication of its kind in the industry. Although it is mostly used by West Coast casting professionals, and therefore lists mostly West Coast actors, more and more New York actors are listing themselves in the APD. A submission in the APD includes name, contact information, guild memberships, ethnic index, appearances in both the printed and internet versions of the Directory, inclusion in The Link (see below), full resume online, one photo per category in the printed version and up to three photos per category online (for an extra charge of $10 each), up to three representative listings in both the web and printed versions. Fees are $75 per category per year. To be listed in the APD, you must be a paid-up member of a performing union. For more information and a submission form, contact *Academy Players Directory*, 133 North Vine Street, Los Angeles, CA, 90028—310-247-3058 or www.playersdirectory.com or www.acadpd.org.

The *Players' Guide New York (PGNY)*, utilized by casting directors, producers, directors and agents when searching for talent and contact information, is the city's "largest and most respected directory of actors." Published annually, this huge volume lists thousands of actors by category (Leading Men/Women, Character Comedians/Comediennes, Child Boys/Girls, Younger Leading Men/Women, Stunt Men/Women, etc.) and includes pictures, contact information, union affiliation, agent representation, ethnicity, age range, and resume (optional). The basic cost (includes one picture) for inclusion in the PGNY is $98, with extra charges for entering more than one category ($57 for the second category, $47 for the third) or for additional photos ($10 each). Players' Guide benefits include being posted on the expanded PGNY website; appearing automatically in searches done on the APD (see above) so that casting directors on both coasts can access information via the internet; adding or updating a resume online at any time; automatic inclusion in The Link (see below), which is used by industry professionals to send and receive submissions through the internet; and discounts provided by vendors with services for performing artists. (Note: To be listed in PGNY, you must be a member of an actors' union or signed with a union franchised agency. For more information and an application, contact Players' Guide at 123 West 44th Street, Suite 2J, New York, NY, 10036, 212-302-9474, or through their website at www.playersguideny.com.

Websites . . . In this age of the internet, more and more industry professionals are turning to the World Wide Web when looking for actors. The net is convenient for them in that it is easy to surf (thus eliminating the tedium of going through scores of pictures and resumes) and is open 24 hours. Websites are equally convenient for actors—a basic website is easy and inexpensive to create and host (just type "cheap website" in your browser and up will pop hundreds of low-cost, self-building sites) and can contain whatever you'd like agents and casting directors to see and know about you, including your picture, resume, production shots, biographical information, streaming video of work in film, TV and commercials, voice-over demos, reviews, etc. If industry people want to learn more about you, they can do so instantly by going to your website. (Note: If you have a site, be sure to include its web address on your resume and marketing materials.)

Speaking of the World Wide Web, **The Link,** created by the *Academy Players Directory* in partnership with Breakdown Services, allows agents to submit actors to casting directors via the internet. As of June 2000, The Link also connects casting people with members of the PGNY over the WWW. How does it work? The Link allows agents to electronically review each breakdown of available roles, then instantly submit an actor's name, resume and photo to the casting director. Moreover, The Link allows casting directors the ability to view actor video and audio demo reels. Inclusion in The Link is free as long as the actor is listed in either the PGNY or the APD.

(Note: The sample mailings I've included in this chapter are just that, samples, and are not intended for you to copy. Use them as you would a template to inspire you and to spark your imagination when creating your own personalized cover letter, press mailing, postcard message, etc.)

Training

The will to win is important, but the will to prepare is vital.

JOE PATERNO

Acting Class

Early in my acting training, a teacher said to me, "For a very few actors, it's 90 percent inspiration and 10 percent perspiration. For the rest of us, it's the other way around—90 percent perspiration, 10 percent inspiration." For all but a handful of actors, talent is not conferred at birth. It does not magically descend from above. The seeds of talent are in each of us, of course, or we most likely would not be doing this, but we have to work hard and do a lot of perspiring to hone our craft. The best way to do that is to study.

A class is the place where you can flex your acting muscles and learn, improve and enrich your skills and keep them well oiled when you are "between engagements." It provides a foundation for your work and helps you create your own technique. It can boost your confidence; if you're going through a "dry spell," good work in class can empower you. It also allows you the opportunity to work on roles you would not be cast in in the real world, correct performance problems and work on acting habits you want to purge. And it is an ideal networking source: your teachers, coaches, even fellow classmates are all potential future employers or may introduce you to people who are able to offer you work.

Feel like you've mastered what it is you do? Explore other

areas of the profession that you are not familiar with and expand your marketability. You may have perfected your technique but not had much experience doing commercials; take a commercial class. You may give a great monologue audition but your cold reading skills suck; take a cold reading class. You've worked a lot in front of a camera but have had no real stage training? Take a technique class. Always wanted to dance but have two left feet? Take a dance class. Dogs howl whenever you sing? Take a voice lesson.

Most great artists, musicians, actors, dancers and singers continually push themselves to new levels of artistry through study. Why shouldn't you? The best athletes require constant practice and training. Again, why shouldn't you? To have the edge in this competitive business, you have to be at the top of your form. Developing your skills, perfecting your technique and challenging yourself in class are the ways to achieve that.

Where to Study

In New York, there are countless classes covering every aspect of the performing arts, and countless schools that offer them. (For a list of what are considered some of the city's better schools, see the "Training Institutions" section of the "Index of Actor Resources and Services.") Find a class that supports, challenges and excites you. The best way to do that is to do your research. Ask friends about the classes they're enrolled in. Query actors whose work you respect where they are studying. Check out prospective schools over the internet. Meet teachers. Audit classes. Finding a good teacher is like finding a mate—you'll want to "date" as many as you can by meeting with them and auditing their classes until you find the perfect match.

Finding a Teacher/Actor Training Institution Checklist

☑ Do an internet search of prospective schools.

☑ Research prospective teachers: what are his or her qualifications, experience, years teaching, and affiliated institutions?

☑ Ask friends and colleagues about the teachers they train with, the schools they attend.

☑ Contact actors whose work you connect with and ask where they study.

☑ Ask the agents and industry people you know which classes come recommended.

☑ Meet with prospective teachers.

☑ Audit prospective classes. Is the teacher's style and curriculum appealing to you and the way you like to train? What is the quality of the students' work?

☑ Find out the cost and size of prospective classes.

☑ Attend an "Open House" or sample class day at prospective institutions.

☑ What are your instincts telling you about the teacher and school? Do both provide a creative and supportive atmosphere?

Agents

What They Do

The most important people in our professional lives are our agents. Ultimately, we can't get ahead in this business without them. They are our protectors, career-molders, hand-holders, champions, advocates and mentors. They are responsible for seeking employment opportunities for clients, submitting actors to and obtaining auditions from casting directors, offering career guidance, negotiating salaries and contracts, developing talent and guiding futures. Because they are essentially employment agencies for actors, they must be licensed. Most agencies are franchised by the three major acting unions (AEA, AFTRA and SAG), which means they have to meet the ethical and professional standards established by each union to be allowed to represent their membership. (If you're not a union member, you may still work with a franchised agency; however if you are in any of the acting unions, you must only work with an agency that is franchised. If you are uncertain about an agency's union affiliation, call the union in question and inquire.) Contrary to what you might think, agents cannot get you an acting job—that's up to you, your craft, talent, ability, reputation and audition skills. What an agent can do is introduce you to the people who employ actors; it's then your job to get those people to hire you. Think of talent agents this way: If an actor is the "commodity" and the casting person, producer or director the "consumer," the agent is the "salesperson."

For the work they've done on your behalf, agents are entitled to a 10 percent commission on all monies you receive, to be paid to them only after you've been paid. Occasionally the commission will be deducted from your paycheck and forwarded to your agency by your employer. More often than not, you will be required to send the commission to your agents on an agreed upon schedule (weekly or monthly). To maintain goodwill with your agency, pay your percentage in full and on time. (Note: Agencies are not permitted by regulations to take more than a ten percent commission; if they ask for more, contact your union. Also, if an agency asks you for commissions or fees upfront, they are in violation of union rules; again, contact your union.)

An actor can work with an agency in one of two ways: either by "freelancing" or becoming a "signed client." If you are freelance, this means you have no contractual agreement with any one agency and may work with as many different agencies as you like. The positive side of freelancing is that by working with a couple to several agencies, over a period of time it will become clear who is most interested in and working hardest for you, and who you will ultimately want to sign with. Negatively, freelance clients are usually the last to get calls from agents, and since there is no contractual obligation, agents tend not to commit as much time and energy to them.

Being a signed client means you consent to work exclusively with one agency in the agreed upon area of the business for which you have signed a contract (commercials, legit or both). Ultimately, signing is what you will want to do. For its signed clients, an agency commits the bulk of its energies, resources and time to not only helping them find work, but nurturing and developing their careers. This does not mean you cannot have different agencies for different areas of the business—one for commercial, one for stage, TV and film, etc.—for the reason that agencies specialize in different fields.

In your dealings with agents, always be courteous and professional. Being demanding, arrogant or a diva (or divo) will only get you the boot when it comes time for the agency's annual "house-cleaning" (and most agencies do it). Trust that an agent is looking out for your best interests and heed his or her suggestions and advice. It's all right to disagree with them, but to have arrived in their positions, they've probably been around "the business" block a few times and deserve the benefit of the doubt and to be allowed to explain their reasoning. If your disagreements become profound, you can try to resolve your issues through either consultation with your union or arbitration. If worse comes to worst, you may sever ties with the agency by making a couple of quick calls and by writing short letters to the agency and to your talent unions.

Never drop in on or call your agent (or their assistants for that matter) to talk about the weather or to ask, "What's going on?" Always have a reason. Interrupting their busy day with inane or insignificant questions or observations (often done by actors who fear their agents have forgotten them and think that calling or stopping by is a way to put themselves in front of them), keeps them from doing their job, which is to work for you. If you want to chat with your agent, invite him or her for coffee, a drink or a meal outside of office hours.

You can make it easy to be reached by being sure that your agents have your correct contact information; if they can't get ahold of you, you may miss out on an audition. Not being able to reach you will anger your agent, no doubt leave him or her with the feeling that you're irresponsible or don't take your career very seriously, and maybe cause the agent to put out less effort on your behalf. When your agent leaves a message about an audition, always call back as soon as possible to confirm all the details. Whenever you will be out of town or unavailable for auditions or work, give your agents your departure and return dates. This way, your agent won't spend precious time working on auditions you won't be able to attend.

Finally, a talent agency is a business established not only to look after its clients, but to MAKE MONEY. They make money only when you make money. To garner your agent's attention and respect, work hard on your craft and audition skills, book work, and earn money for the both of you.

How to Meet Them

In the beginning of your career, you may not want to immediately focus all your attention on finding an agent. For the most part, agents are looking to represent actors who have some experience and professional or semi-professional credits. Without these, an agent will be reluctant to work with you. Instead of wasting long hours and lots of sweat pursuing them right away, expend the hours and sweat trying to find as much work as you can, in as many venues as you can. Once you feel your resume and your skills reflect a sufficient body of work and experience, you will be ready to go agent hunting.

Keep in mind that with so many of us (that 90,000 figure once again) vying for their attention, time and energy, finding an agent is a Herculean effort. There are several ways to go about pursuing representation, but do yourself a favor and go into the process with your eyes open, knowing that it will probably be the biggest challenge of your career. I'll reiterate: Don't go looking for an agent until you are ready. If you are fortunate enough to be invited to meet an agent and audition for him or her but your audition skills are untested and your craft not quite developed, you'll get no further than the first meeting, and may never be invited back again.

● The number one way an agent finds an actor is by **seeing them work**. Agents are always looking for new clients and the best way for them to do that is to attend plays, showcases, workshops, and scene nights, which they do regularly. Get yourself into as many of these as possible, do good work, invite agents to come see you and cross your fingers and hope they, one, show up, and two, like what they see. (Note: At the end of each performance of the play, scene night, workshop or show-case you're doing, be sure to ask the box office for a list of the agents that were in the house. You will want to follow up with each by sending a note reminding them where they saw you along with a picture and resume or postcard and your contact information.)

● Agents will often meet performers that come **recommended** to them by actors who are their signed clients, as well as casting directors, directors, producers, writers and other industry peo-ple. To approach these people about referring you to an agent, you should know them well and have auditioned for or worked with them so that they are familiar with your abilities. Since by recommending you their reputations (not to mention taste and discernment) are on the line, they will only do so if they know you, know what you can do, and agree you'd be a good match with that particular agent.

● Doing a **mass mailing** in which you target several agents to send your picture and resume to can often open doors for you. *If* your picture and resume land on an agent's desk, and *if* he or she connects with something that they see, they *may* call you in for an initial interview and/or an audition. Usually the only way this works is if you have a lot of luck and timing on your side, as well as a knockout picture and resume. Why? Almost always, the person who opens the mail at an agency is a recep-tionist or intern who often knows little or nothing about acting or talent. This person goes through each day's batch of pic-tures, selects the very few they like (often with their only crite-rion being, I kid you not, "He's cute," "What dreamy eyes she has," "I like her blouse," "She reminds me of my mother," "He's a hottie") and passes them on to the agents. Where do the rest of the pictures go? If you said, "trash bin," ding, ding, ding, you win the prize. This is why having a great picture and resume, and sending them out all the time, is so important. (For a deeper exploration of this, see the "Headshots," "Resumes" and "Mailings and Marketing" chapters.)

● Try attending one of the many **"Meet the Pros" events**, which are sponsored by several acting schools and performance career oriented organizations. For a fee, these groups provide actors the opportunity to meet and audition for agents.

What you don't want to do is stop by an agent's office. I know a lot of books on the business and acting career gurus encourage actors to do "the rounds": to go from one agency to another dropping off pictures and resumes in the hope of bumping into an agent, engaging him or her in a conversation and being discovered. I'm here to tell you that every agent I know finds it annoying, time-consuming and a distraction from their busy schedules. Coming off as annoying, time-consuming and distracting are not very positive ways to begin a courtship, or to endear you to an agency. Don't go to an agent's office unless you've been invited.

What They Look For

Although there is no one type that an agent is looking for, there are several qualities they seek in the actors they choose to represent. Primarily, they are looking for talent. With so many people wanting to be actors these days, most agents are searching for actors who can act; who can create a character that is truthful and exciting. Experience and training are also important to an agent;

he or she seeks those who have developed their skills and craft to give them a competitive edge.

Beyond this, being easy to work with is a big plus. Not only is an agent assessing you as a potential client and actor, they also want assurances that you'll come off positively and work well with producers, directors, casting people and others in the industry. Their reputations are at stake here.

Actors with game plans for their careers are also appealing—actors who:

- Have a sense of their type and place in "the business"

- Understand how the business works

- Are ambitious (but not Macbeth-like)

- Know what they want and are proactive about attaining it

It also doesn't hurt actors' chances of getting into an agent's good graces by being passionate about what they do, charming, personable, confident, professional, warm, pleasant, intelligent, relaxed, open, desperation-free, and attractive. Finally, agents want to work with well-rounded actors who have lives, interests and concerns outside of their careers. So, stop eating, sleeping and drinking the business, and get out there and enjoy your life and this great city around you.

Before You Sign

Once you begin generating interest from agents, do not sign with anyone until you've done your homework. Find out as much as you can about the agency: Whom do they represent? Who are the other agents in the office? Do the unions franchise them? Are they so big that they don't have time to adequately represent you? Are they so small and unknown an entity that they don't get many calls from casting people? How long have they been in operation? Are they in agreement with you as to your type and how to market you?

Ask yourself whether or not working with the agent would be pleasurable. Signing with an agent is like a marriage: you wouldn't marry just anyone, right? You'd want to go through a period of courtship in order to find out as much as you can about that person. You'd want to know whether or not you are compatible. The same applies to your relationship with your agent. Don't commit unless you are sure that your partnership will be beneficial to both of you.

Take the Reins

Even when you have signed with an agent, don't rely solely on your agent to find you work. Just because you have representation does not mean that your career is instantly made. You still need to work hard and be a proactive participant in your career. You need to know how the business works, who the powers that be are. You need to make and nurture contacts. You need to generate work on your own by going to auditions that you find through the trade papers, networking with friends and fellow actors, and perusing union bulletin boards.

Get involved with readings of new plays; go to industry parties; let "the business" know when you are working; send out reviews of your recent work (if they're favorable, naturally); keep your mailing lists up-to-date; contact people you've collaborated with in the past to see if they are working on new productions; don't be afraid to ask friends and colleagues for help.

Do let your agents know if you hear of an audition that you're right for but are not being seen for; perhaps it did not occur to them to submit you. They occasionally need to be *gently* nudged. Do not stop working at your career because you have people that are doing that for you. By taking the reins of your career, you are not only improving your chances for success, you will also inspire your agents to work harder for you.

Casting Directors

What They Do

The job of the casting director is multifaceted. Contrary to what some cynical actors think, their duties consist of a lot more than just "making phone calls." I'll walk you through what it is they do: A casting director is hired to cast a project. He or she then has to pore over the script to suss out character qualities and determine the types of actors needed for each role. They list the roles being cast and types being sought and send it either directly to agents or to Breakdown Services, a clearinghouse that disseminates this information via the internet to talent agencies. Once the agents have responded by sending pictures and resumes of the actors they feel would be appropriate for each role, the casting director goes through these and selects the actors they'd like to see. They get back to the agents and give them appointment times for their clients' auditions. Next, they take care of the logistical aspects of the audition: lining up a reader to read with the actors and booking studio space (if they don't own it themselves) where the audition will be held.

Finally, during the audition itself, in which the director and/or producer selects the actors they feel best fit the roles they are seeking, more times than not the casting director will be in the room watching the audition as well. After this initial audition, it is the casting director's job to set up callback appointments with the handful of actors the director would like to see again. Once the director chooses whom he wants in each role, the casting person contacts the actors' agents and makes the offers. Often, if a director is waffling about a particular actor or can't make a definitive choice, the casting director will assist in the selection process by offering opinions, assessments and anecdotes about the actors being considered. Frequently, the director or producer will ask the casting director to negotiate the terms of the contract with the actor's agent.

To be effective in their jobs, casting directors need to know the talent pool inside and out and to continually be looking for new actors. So, they spend a lot of time seeing theater and showcases, going to films and watching television and demo reels. In the off-season (the summer and late December to early January), many casting directors will hold general interviews and/or auditions to meet new talent.

A casting director is only as good as the actors he or she puts before the industry. The credibility and success they achieve with directors and producers is dependent on the ability and talent of the actors they bring into the audition room. That means you the actor have got to be ready and know what you're doing. If you blow it, you may not get a second chance to redeem yourself. Besides everything else you need to accomplish in an audition, part of your job is to make the casting director look good by being good. If you don't, the director may question the casting person's taste and discernment, and possibly will not hire him or her again. In turn, the casting person will, understandably, be angry and never or rarely ever bring you back; they may even share your ineptitude with others in the industry.

Given the importance and position of casting directors in our lives (not to mention the control they have over our careers and futures), I can't stress vehemently enough that you should always be kind and courteous in your encounters with them. Moreover, try to keep the quality of your auditions consistently high. When you look good, casting directors look good, and if you make them look good, they'll keep bringing you back.

How To Meet Them

The best way to meet a casting director is **through an agent**. If you don't have one, don't despair, there are a few other ways to get seen.

- **Send a picture and resume** to a casting director **for a specific project**; it may on occasion elicit a response. If they can't find what they are looking for in the agent submissions they've received, they will sometimes go through the pile of unsolicited pictures. If you happen to be what they're looking for and timing and luck are on your side, they may very well call you. So, by all means, send your picture and resume to them.

- Depending on how busy they are, casting people will periodically **meet those referred to them** through actors they respect or other industry people. That's why networking, as well as not burning any bridges, is so important.

- Several organizations throughout the city host **"Meet the Pros" events**, where, for a fee, you can meet and/or audition for casting people. Don't like the idea of paying to meet the industry? I agree it sounds dubious, but it works; I know lots of actors who got their first breaks attending these when they had no other way to meet casting directors.

- **Consider taking a class with a casting person**. It's often a great way for an actor to be seen, and, if they like you, they're apt to bring you in on the projects they're working on.

- If they attend **a play, workshop or showcase that you're appearing in** and like what they see, they may call you for a meet-and-greet or an audition. So, get into as many productions, no matter how small or out of the way they are. (Note: As I said in the chapter "Agents," if you do a showcase, make sure to ask the box office at the end of each night for a list of industry people that were in the house. You'll want to follow up with them with a note attached to your picture and resume.)

No matter what, do not call or drop by the offices of these people unless they are expecting you, even if it's just to leave off a picture and resume. They are very busy and can't be bothered by an unannounced visit. (Just imagine the chaos there'd be if only a fraction of the 90,000 actors in the city decided to pay a call on them.) It's a sure-fire way to alienate casting directors, which is the opposite of what you want to do.

The Audition

Like it or not (and, for your sake, I hope you learn to love it), auditioning is about the only way to get work in our competitive profession. We all have to do it. Even established "name" actors and bona fide stars have to periodically read for roles. It's our equivalent to the real world's job interview, except that we will be doing it a whole hell of a lot more (sometimes every day, sometimes several times a day) than 99 percent of the "lay" population. Given the huge number of actors in New York and the dearth of roles and work, the pressure to audition well is great. It's that pressure that makes the audition so feared and loathed.

How can you alleviate audition anxiety? First, have a good understanding of all the different types of auditions there are (more about this anon) and the different techniques each requires. Second, make sure you are well prepared. An audition is a mini-performance and, like with a play, the better rehearsed you are the less anxious you will feel, no matter whether you are in front of 3,000 spectators in an outdoor amphitheater or a director and casting person in a five-by-five hovel in the middle of midtown. The audition bottom line is: the more familiar you are with the entire process, the more relaxed and unintimidated you will be.

Getting Auditions

Once you have become established, most of your auditions will come through your agents (commercial auditions will almost always be set up by an agent). In the meantime, there are a few sources through which you may find auditions. The most popular way is through **weekly trade papers and magazines** like

Backstage, Show Business Weekly, and *Variety.* (For a full description of these, see the "Index of Actor Resources and Services.") Bulletin boards at the actors' unions AEA, SAG and AFTRA (see "Index of Actor Resources and Services" for these addresses) list auditions, as do internet sites such as www.actorsny.com, www.castinglist.com, and www.thebuzz.com. Networking with friends and colleagues is also a good way to find out what is being cast; don't be afraid to ask what they are auditioning for or what they've heard about. Just remember: turn about is fair play; if you are going to ask others about their auditions, you should be willing to share information about yours as well.

Types of Auditions

You will encounter five types of auditions:

1. The Open Call, a.k.a. "Cattle Call"

The "open call," advertised in trade papers, on audition websites and the AEA bulletin board, gives actors (usually those who don't have agents or who have not yet established reputations for themselves) the opportunity to audition for and be seen by members of the industry. Such auditions, which are open to anyone who wishes to attend, are referred to as "cattle calls" because hundreds of actors often turn out for them. That means there's a wide range of experience, from absolute amateur to seasoned veteran, queuing for their two to three minutes of getting-seen time (if you're good, you're sure to stand out). That also means that the lines begin forming very early in the morning and are very long (do yourself a favor and go with a folding chair, reading material, Gameboy, laptop, food, drink and whatever else you'll need to get through this ordeal). Because there are so many actors who attend open calls, not everyone will be seen. The earlier you arrive, the better your chances are of auditioning.

Sounds bleak, eh? Look at it this way: Your job, especially early in your career, is to meet as many industry people as you can and to fine-tune your audition technique. The open call is the way to do both.

2. The Scheduled Audition Appointment

The "scheduled" audition appointment is almost always arranged by an agent and conducted by a casting director—which is why an agent is devoutly to be wished for. How it works is, a casting director informs agents, usually through Breakdown Services (see "Take Control" and "Index of Actor Resources and Services" for more information), of the role or roles being cast. The agent responds by sending the casting director the pictures and resumes of all clients they represent that may be appropriate. The casting director goes through these submissions and selects those actors they wish to see. They then contact the agents to set up appointments. Not having agent representation does not preclude your being seen; it just may be a little harder. You may hear of a project that is being cast and feel you'd be spot-on for the role, so send the casting director your picture and resume. If you're lucky, he or she will see a quality in either or both that would be ideal for the role and bring you in.

If you are not granted an appointment, do not try to crash the audition; this will anger the casting director and guarantee they will not see you ever again. Exceptions such as the following prove the rule: Years ago, a major musical was being cast. The agents of a well-known actress lobbied to have their client seen for a pivotal role, but kept being turned down by the casting office. As luck would have it, the actress was invited to a party where the director of the musical was the honored guest. The actress introduced herself to the director, told him of her inability to get an audition and asked the director if he would see her. He said yes and she showed up at the audition the following Monday. Before the actress went in, the casting director who had refused to see her came out and told her, "You went above my head to get this audition. I just want you to know that after today, you will never be back in my office again." The actress auditioned, and, as I'm sure you've guessed, got the part. Being in the show raised her profile and, naturally, she was brought back to audition through that particular casting office many more times. This was a happy ending to a potentially career-killing episode, but don't be lulled into thinking that similar behavior will always get such a positive result. Don't crash an audition unless you're willing to deal with the backlash.

3. The Monologue Audition

There are three audition scenarios in which a monologue may be required: for stage auditions; when showing agents who are interested in working with you what you've got; or at open calls. It is rare, if ever, that you will be asked to do a monologue for film, TV or commercial work. A "monologue" audition is exactly that—an audition with a speech, most often pulled from a play or film, that is performed solo. You should have at least two contrasting pieces prepared, one comic, one dramatic. Having four monologues in your back pocket would be even better: contemporary comic and dramatic, classical comic and dramatic. Rehearse each of them thoroughly. Work on them with coaches or friends. Make them truthful and exciting. Do not—repeat, do not—present a monologue that is only partially prepared or learned the night before. You get so few chances in this business to show what you can do; if your piece is half-baked, you may not get a chance to redeem yourself. (Note: While doing your monologue, even if it's a "direct address" piece [when a character speaks directly to the audience], do not look at your auditors. You will only make them uncomfortable, because they'll feel compelled to respond in some way and they won't be able to objectively assess your work. Place the focus of your piece just above and to the side of the heads of your auditors.

4. The Callback

After the initial audition, the director usually brings back a handful of actors for a second (and sometimes a third, fourth and fifth) look or "callback." At the callback, you'll be asked to read again, probably the same material as your initial audition, as well as a new scene. You may also be paired with another actor to see what you look like together and how you relate to each other. For your callback, go wearing exactly what you had on at the initial audition. Those who are calling you back liked both your acting and the way you looked; give them again what they liked. Also, by wearing the same outfit, you help them remember your first audition. The callback is an important step to landing a job; if you've been called back, you are under serious consideration for the role, so go as if the role is yours . . . fully prepared and confident.

5. The Commercial Audition

Commercial work is one of the most remunerative areas of our profession. Landing a long-running national network or "Class A" spot (a commercial that sponsors a television program on a network and plays in twenty or more cities) could easily net $30,000 to $40,000 or more. How? Why? Each and every time the spot airs, you are paid a handsome use-fee (a residual for a commercial). If it shows a lot, you are paid a lot.

Because commercials are so lucrative, the competition to book them, as you can imagine, is fierce. There is a rule about commercials that's been bouncing around the business probably since television's inception that says you need to do a hundred commercial auditions to land one. Knowing how to effectively audition for commercials will help you do just that.

To give successful "commercial" auditions (and to appear to know the commercial audition routine), there are several procedures you should know and follow. First, when you arrive at the casting office, sign in on the sheet provided, write your name, phone number, agent contact, call and arrival times, ethnicity, and, if under eighteen, your age. Next, fill out a size card, which asks for name, address, agency, and all sizes. The information on this card is used by producers to contact you and, since commercials are done very quickly, to give the costumer a head start on assembling your wardrobe. Be sure you know all your measurements, including hat and glove sizes. After the size card is filled out, have your Polaroid taken and stapled to the card. Now you can look over the "copy" (the material you've been asked to read for your audition; for commercials, you will not be required to perform a prepared piece such as a monologue), any posted directions, and the "storyboard" (a set of sketches, arranged in sequence on panels, outlining the scenes that make up the story of the commercial) usually taped to the wall right above the sign-in sheet. (Note: Arrive to the commercial audition earlier—anywhere from ten to twenty minutes—than your scheduled appointment to give yourself adequate time to fully review the storyboard and familiarize yourself with the copy.)

When your name is called, enter the audition room and go straight to your "mark," which is usually a large "X" or "T" taped to the floor. This is where you will stand for your audition. You will be asked to "slate," which in layman's terms means to state your name. Do this *personably* and *clearly*. More often than not, when the commercial's director, advertising executives and client representatives (those people representing the company that is sponsoring the ad) review the audition tape, they will only have time to look at the slate portion of the session (usually one to two hundred actors audition for a commercial spot, making it virtually impossible to go through each individual audition).

Often you'll be asked to show your profiles. Since in commercials the look of an actor is very important (after all, you'll be representing the product), the client—the product's executives and ad agency, who may be in the audition room—will want to see all sides of your face. Turn your body and face left for a full beat, then do the same to the right. If you are asked to show your hands (in case you're needed to hold the product, the powers that be want to know that your nails are clean and not bitten down to the nubs, and that you have no unsightly warts, scars or marks); hold them together palm side facing you just below your chin, then turn your palms out.

Once this is done, the casting director will possibly give you some direction as to what the ad agency and client are looking for. Listen carefully as you'll be expected to execute this direction. Often you'll be given the chance to rehearse reading the provided copy, improvising the given scenario or doing whatever the audition requires. Attack it as if it was the actual taping. If the casting director gives you an adjustment, do your best to incorporate it into your read. Finally, you'll put your audition down on tape. If you have a lot of text to say, don't worry about memorizing it. Cue cards with the script printed in large bold letters will be provided, usually just to the side of the eye of the camera. Don't be afraid to read from the card as long as you make some contact with the camera or others in the spot.

The most successful commercial auditions are those that are loose, warm and personal. Even if you're auditioning as a product's spokesperson, try not to give it a stiff, stentorian read. Instead, imagine you are speaking to a loved one, telling him or her about the merits and advantages of the product you are plugging. Find the things you adore about the product and why your loved one needs to buy it. This will personalize your read and give it your imprimatur.

Audition Fundamentals

No matter whether you're auditioning for a play, film, soap, sitcom, television drama, commercial or industrial (for the uninitiated, an industrial is a film designed to present selected information about a large industrial enterprise; they are often also in-house training films for corporations for the purpose of teaching employees about company procedures, rules, etc.); no matter whether you're asked to do a monologue, a cold reading (an audition in which an actor reads aloud from a script with little or no rehearsal beforehand; the majority of film, television and commercial auditions are cold readings) or to prepare assigned "sides" (the pages from the script that you'll be reading for your audition, usually given to you by the casting director prior to the audition); no matter if the audition is an open call or a scheduled appointment, there are several basics that, when followed, can help you relax, stay focused and book work:

Do your **research about the director** you are auditioning for. What were his or her past projects? Where did they train? What theaters, studios or television production companies are they affiliated with? What have critics said about their work? (Note: This can be done easily over the internet...just "google" them: go to www.google.com, type in their name, and *voilà!* you'll find everything you need to know.)

Make sure you **have the correct date, time, address and material for your audition**. There is a no bigger turn-off for auditors than late, unprepared actors.

If you're running late for your audition, call ahead or have your agent call. Given the limited time of audition appointments, your late arrival is going to unravel an already tight schedule. By calling ahead, you at least give the auditors a heads up so that they can schedule around you.

If for some reason **you need to cancel an audition appointment**, try to give more than twenty-four hours notice. The casting director will want to fill your slot and need some time to do it (selecting the actor who will take your place and giving that actor enough time to prepare). Think of it this way: if you don't give enough notice, you're keeping another actor from vying for a job. You'll also really piss the casting person off. (Note: Make sure that your reason for canceling is valid and that you do it only in dire or unforeseen situations—death of a family or friend, illness, another job that conflicts with your appointment; canceling too many auditions is a sure recipe for killing your career.)

Go dressed like the character you're auditioning for. That does not mean to wear a costume—that's the best way to shoot yourself in the foot before you even begin to read. Go suggesting your character (see chapter on "Personal Presentation"). If you are called back for a role, wear exactly what you wore in the initial audition.

Arrive at your audition early so that you, relax, catch your breath, meditate, pee, comb you hair, touch up your makeup, go over your material, or whatever else you need to do to prepare. Don't let this time become your social hour. You're sure to run into a gaggle of actors you know; gossiping, catching up or trading recipes will split your focus and diminish your concentration.

Never, never, **never go to an audition without a picture and re-**

sume. Although you are sure your agent already sent one, bring more. You never know if there are other projects you're being considered for, or if the casting director's dog ate the first one.

Almost every audition you do will require you to **sign in**. You'll be asked to give your contact, union and agent information, and, as in the case of commercials, sizes.

Once you've arrived and signed in, **double check to make sure you have the correct audition materials**. There is often a "monitor" who can answer your questions about the audition. Make sure to look over any information that may be provided about the project (either posted or on the sign-in table).

In the theater, there is a rule about **keeping your troubles outside the stage door**; it should be applied to auditions as well. No matter what ails you, leave it outside the audition room or it will color your work. Let your audition be a several-minutes-long vacation from your problems.

Enter the audition room confidently—head up, shoulders back. Go in looking (and feeling) like a winner. Say "hello" to and shake hands with everyone in the room. (For proper meeting and greeting etiquette, see the "Giving Good Interview" chapter.)

Once inside the room, unless you are engaged in conversation, **keep the pre-audition chitchat to a minimum**. As scintillating as you may be, the auditors are short on time (and almost always running late) and they are most interested in whether or not you can act, whether you can play the character. That does not mean you shouldn't be personable, courteous, warm and friendly; they also want to know that spending time with you on a set or in a rehearsal room will be pleasurable.

If there is a line or word in the material you're auditioning with that **you don't understand, look it up**. If you don't know how to pronounce a word, look it up. If you butcher a word or mangle an idea, you'll look none too bright. If you're not too bright and want to work, for your sake, I hope you're beautiful! (Note: The best source for looking up words, of course, is the dictionary, either the old-fashioned book variety or online version. For ideas or concepts that you don't understand, try going to www.askjeeves.com and typing in the line in question. Often several entries will come up for your scrutiny.)

Don't go into the audition room until you are ready. It's all right to ask for another minute or two to look over the material or to get focused.

Don't go in "winging" your audition. It should be fully prepared—the entire script read at least once (if available; if your audition is set up through an agent, he or she will often have a copy of the script available for you to peruse), the character's objectives, intentions, through-line and obstacles worked through and specific choices made.

Having said that, **don't over rehearse** your audition to the point where you kill spontaneity and freshness. You should balance preparing what you're going to do and making and committing to choices, with appearing to be in the moment.

Don't ask the auditors what they are looking for. By asking, you appear lazy and it puts them on the spot: nine times out of ten they don't know what they want until the see it. Give them your interpretation of the role—it just may be exactly what they didn't know they wanted.

Don't try to give the auditor what you think he or she wants. As ours is an interpretive art, the industry wants to see your interpretation of a role. Besides, more often than not, the auditor has no idea what he or she wants until it walks into the room.

Allow for some spontaneity in your audition. If something happens instinctively that seems in character that you hadn't rehearsed, go with it. It may lead you in a different, more inspired direction.

If it is a **cold reading** you are doing, before going into the audition room make and commit to strong choices about the preceding circumstances of the scene you are reading for are, your character's objective, how you feel about what you are saying and how you feel about what is being said to you.

Strive to not only **be truthful** in your audition, but **also exciting**. Don't play it safe. Make dynamic choices. It is the compelling audition that will be remembered and it is the remembered actor who gets the part. However, make sure your choices are organic to your character. If you're outrageous for the sake of leaving an impression, but your choice is not rooted in the character's reality, you'll get points for courage but may leave the auditors thinking either you don't know what you are doing or are a nut job. Moreover, refrain from removing your clothes (don't scoff, more actors than you'd imagine do it as a way to show how brave they are or how "in the moment" they can be). Occasionally nudity is required for a role; if you are auditioning for such a part for a legitimate director, producer, casting person, etc., you will be given notice in advance (and usually asked to undress down to a bathing suit only). There is often a union representative present to monitor the audition.

If during your audition **you lose focus** for a moment, flub a line or do something unintended, **don't let it throw you**. Stop the self-monitoring commentary in your head, let the mistake go and get back to your character's objectives and intentions in the scene. By beating yourself up ("Why did I do that?") or panicking internally, your concentration will diminish, which will read in your audition. If (and only if) you feel that your reading has collapsed into the unsalvageable, stop and ask the auditor if you may start over. This will almost always be allowed. Take a few deep breaths, concentrate on the text and character and, when you feel ready, begin again. (Note: Many casting directors don't like actors to stop and start over—it takes up valuable time. If you must stop, do it only once... you'll be forgiven the first time, written off the second.)

If something throws you or you lose your place in the script, **stay in character** as you recover or find the line you lost.

Be prepared to do an audition more than one way. After your initial reading, the director may ask you to make an adjustment, which, hopefully, he or she will make clear. (A director actually once said to me in an audition, "That was okay, but it was very 'yellow.' I want more 'blue.' " Cross my heart and hope to die, this really happened.) Don't be so rigid in your interpretation that you can't easily make the change. If you disagree, don't argue with or try to dissuade the director; this is the best guarantee for not getting the job. Usually when a director does this, he or she is interested in you and wants to see if you are adaptable, if you can take direction. Do your best to make the adjustment. If after the director's note you're still not clear what he or she is looking for, don't hesitate to ask that the direction be clarified.

In most of your auditions, you'll be reading with another person. That person could be a "reader" hired specifically by a casting director to read with all who are auditioning, a fellow actor who is up for a role in the same project, or the casting director (this often happens in film and TV auditions). Always **connect with the person you're reading with**. Get your focus out of the script as much as possible and look into the reader's eyes. Feed off what he or she is giving you. If your reader gives you a whole lot of nothing (and trust me, you'll encounter a whole lot of them—their eyes buried in the script, their delivery dull, dry or just plain bad), don't get mad or frustrated. This will surely show in your audition. Instead, endow the reader with all the qualities you need them to have to do good work. No matter how bad they are, imagine they are giving you exactly what you want and need.

You will occasionally be asked **to audition for a piece that you don't like**. As much as you hate the part or script, you may feel compelled to accept the audition (to pay bills, accrue insurance weeks, gain weeks for unemployment, etc.). You have only two choices: turn down the audition, or find something in the script that you love and give it your best shot. If you don't, you won't be able to adequately mask your disdain, which will be perceptible in your audition.

You should **become very familiar with your lines** but **you don't need to learn them cold**; your interpretive skills, not your memorization skills, are being judged. There is always the possibility you'll forget a line (there's no one to feed you a line if you "go up"), then focus on it and toss the audition. There's also another possibility that you'll come off as if you have completely created the role, made all the decisions, done all the work and have no room to grow. To illustrate: I once went to an audition with all my lines learned and planned perfectly. As I finished, the director, who had a sour look on his face, said sarcastically, "Well, Craig, I

guess if I cast you, I don't have to bring you in until tech week...
you've done all my work for me." I didn't get the job.

The only time **it is probably a good idea to have your lines
learned is for on-camera auditions** (film and TV roles). Because
you'll most likely be filmed in close-up, constantly moving your
eyes from the page to the reader can be distracting. Moreover,
since film and TV both happen so quickly (you're usually cast
only a few days before you actually shoot), the directors, producers and casting people want to be assured that you will have no
problem learning lines.

**If you're doing a musical audition, have at least two songs pre-
pared** (up tempo and ballad), preferably in the style of the show
you're auditioning for. Each page of your sheet music should be
taped together or the pages made easy to turn. Your music should
be written in your key and legible.

At the end of your audition, **don't ask, "How did I do?"** (Do I
even need to explain to you why this is wrong?) Moreover, during
your audition, **don't look at the auditors to try and gauge their
reactions** to your work. This makes them uncomfortable and appears as if you're asking them, "How'm I doing?" Or worse, "Do
I get the job?"

Don't apologize or make excuses (i.e., being late or unprepared,
giving a bad read, flubbing a line, etc.). By doing so, you lower
your status with the auditors. They are looking for actors who are
confident and on top of their game; being contrite will send the
opposite message.

When you have finished, thank the auditors and exit as you came
in... **like a winner**. Even if you think your audition didn't go very

well, walk out with the attitude that you just nailed it; a positive demeanor and upright body language may convince the auditors that you nailed your audition as well.

Once you're out of the audition room, **drag your heels** a little before exiting the building. With you outside the room, the auditors might confer and desire to see more of you on the spot. They may want to pair you up with another actor or have you read other material. If you're still outside the room or in the building, they can easily track you down and bring you back in. Every actor I know has had the experience of being followed out to the lobby, stopped before entering an elevator, or even chased down the street by a casting director wanting to see more of his or her work.

Don't view your audition as an opportunity to obtain work; instead, **think of your audition as a short performance,** a chance to show the auditor what you can do. This will take the onus off of your employment-needy side and tap into your creative side.

Rejection

Rejection is part of the process of being an actor. It happens to the best of us, and all the time. If you are at all thin-skinned, you should probably think about some other profession NOW. Keep in mind, however, that not getting a role doesn't mean that the director didn't like you, or that the casting director thought your audition was wretched. Many things are factored into casting that often have nothing to do with talent. You may look too young (or too old) for the part. You may not be the right height, have the desired hair color or skin tone. You may not "fit" with the actor already cast to play opposite the character you're auditioning for. You may remind the director of his ex-wife who bankrupted him before fleeing to the Bahamas with the mailman. There are a million reasons why you may not be cast, most of which have nothing to do with talent. So, don't overanalyze why you weren't cast and don't assume that the reason you didn't get a part was because you were dismissed as talent-free. If you feel like you nailed an audition and can't understand why you weren't cast, ask your agent to get some feedback from the director or casting person. (Note: Be sparing in your request for feedback; if you do it too many times, you will become a nuisance.) After each rejection, do like the song and pick yourself up, brush yourself off and audition all over again.

Every Audition Is an Education

Do as many auditions as you can. Each and every one is part of your learning process and the more you do, the more comfortable and the better you will be at doing them. By the same token, if you blow an audition, don't beat yourself up. Determine what it is you need to do to improve and move on. Don't dwell on what you did wrong. Continually overanalyzing your mistakes will heighten them to the point that you will fail before you enter the audition room. Instead, think about what you will do right next time.

Audition Checklist

☑ Research the director, producer and theater you are auditioning for.

☑ Go to your audition *suggesting* your character, but don't go so far as to wear a costume.

☑ Arrive early to do what you need to prepare.

☑ Don't forget to bring a picture and resume. Even if you're sure they have one, bring another.

☑ Sign in and double check to make sure you have the correct audition materials.

☑ Leave the woes of your personal life outside the audition room.

☑ Enter the room confidently. Be warm and friendly, say "hello" and shake hands with all of the auditors. When you've finished, thank them and exit like a winner.

☑ Keep the chitchat with the auditors to a minimum.

☑ Go in prepared—do your homework. What are the character's objectives, intentions, actions, and obstacles? Make specific choices.

☑ Don't overprepare so that your audition loses spontaneity.

☑ Make dynamic choices that are organic to your character.

☑ If you make mistakes during your audition, let them go. Likewise, if the audition devolves into helplessness, stop and ask if you may begin again; don't ask a second time.

☑ Make sure you understand everything that you are saying in an audition. Ignorance may be bliss, but it won't land you a job.

☑ Be prepared to do your audition more than one way—don't be so rigid in your interpretation that you can't do it any other way if asked.

☑ Allow for spontaneity; if something inspired happens, go with it.

☑ Connect with the reader, feed off what he or she is giving you. If they are no good, endow them with the qualities you need to make your audition a success.

☑ If you don't like the piece you're asked to audition for, either turn it down or find something redeemable about it.

☑ Be very familiar with your lines, but don't memorize them (unless you are auditioning for a film or television role).

☑ Give the director your interpretation of the role, not what you *think* his or her concept is.

☑ For your monologue auditions, have four contrasting pieces prepared that you can draw from—contemporary dramatic, comic, classical comic and dramatic.

☑ For musical auditions, prepare two songs—up-tempo and ballad; make sure your music is attached, written in your key and legible.

☑ For commercial auditions, make sure you know the entire routine—signing in, filling out a size card, getting your Polaroid taken, finding your mark, slating, showing your profiles and hands, reading from the provided cue cards, and making your "read" warm and personal as if you were talking to a loved one.

☑ Make sure you have the correct date, time, place and material for your audition.

☑ Call ahead if you are running late for an audition. It's a courtesy to your auditors whose schedule is very tight.

☑ If you need to cancel an audition, give the casting director enough notice so that he or she can find another actor to take your spot.

☑ Don't view your audition as an employment opportunity. Think of it as a chance to do what you do best—perform.

Giving Good
Interview

Poll one hundred actors on what their least favorite part of the business is, and the majority would say, "interviewing." Unfortunately, this bane of ours is a necessary evil. Often in the process of finding representation or securing an acting job, we are required to interview with potential agents, employers and collaborators. The interview is one of the few opportunities that directors, agents, producers and casting people have to get to know you one-on-one. It's important in that it lets these people get a glimpse at who you are. You may have demonstrated through your talent that you're the "Next Big Thing," tomorrow's "It Girl" (or boy), but those capable of employing you or helping you find work also want to know if you are interesting, charming, warm, personable, intelligent, funny and confident. A tall order.

The agent/client relationship is like a marriage, with the interview being the first date, the "getting to know you" rite of passage in which they'll determine if they want to invest years of time and energy on your behalf, and vice versa. Directors, producers and casting people not only use the interview as a way to suss out similarities between you and the role they are trying to cast, but also as a means to determine whether or not you'll be enjoyable to spend time with on a set or in a rehearsal room, and if you have the potential of being a freak or a pain in the ass.

Meeting with the "Powers That Be"

Meeting with an industry person is a big deal. Industry people are very busy and have little time to interview actors. Getting the appointment itself is big. The agent, director, producer or casting person has responded to your picture, resume, cover letter or all three, has contacted you to come in for a meeting, and is taking time out of his or her busy schedule to chat with you. They want you to come in and solve their problems. They want you to be exceptional. They perhaps even want to see dollar signs when you walk in the door.

What are they looking for? Several things: Do you listen? Are you relaxed? Are you yourself? Can you keep the conversation buoyant? Are you spontaneous? Can you think on your feet? Are you positive? Enthusiastic? They also want to see how you behave under pressure and if you present yourself at all negatively—are you cocky? Self-centered? A blowhard? A gossip? A whiner?

For the most part, actors hate the interview process because it is unscripted. I hear over and over, "Put some text in my hands, give me a character to work on, and I'm fine; but if I have to go in and be myself, I become a babbling idiot." That's because more often than not, we go into the interview "winging it." Being unprepared, we become tongue-tied, our hearts race faster than if we were running a marathon, cotton takes up residence in our mouths, our brains feel like they are about to explode, and inanities come tumbling out of us. A friend loves to tell the story of an interview he had early in his career, where, in an awkward pause, he blurted to the woman he was meeting with, "nice nylons." Cringe! I'll bet a lot of us have similar anecdotes.

Do Your Homework

The best way to insure that you will be cool, relaxed and in good form during your interview is to go prepared. Before the interview, find out as much as you can about the person you are meeting with. Ask your friends and colleagues what they know about this person. Do an internet search by typing his or her name into your web browser. If you are to meet an agent, call Equity and ask the names of some of the actors they represent. If it's a casting director, research past work he or she has done as well as current and future projects. As the adage goes, "knowledge is power," and the more you know about the person you're interviewing with, the more powerful and comfortable you'll feel.

Practice Makes Perfect

From beginning to end, what you do and say in an interview should be as rehearsed as an audition. Practice how you're going to enter and exit the room (standing tall, open, proud, confident); your handshake (firm but not aggressive—no lifeless, limp hands, please); how you sit (with ease and grace); how you conduct yourself. (My agent Nancy Curtis tells a story about a young actor whom she'd seen at a student showcase. She liked his work and called him in for a meeting in which he spent the entire time sucking on a lollipop. That's all she remembered about him, and subsequently she was not interested in representing him.)

Have answers prepared to the inevitable questions that all industry people ask:

- What have you done lately?

- What do you think your "type" is?

- Who in "the business" do you know and who have you met?

- Where did you train?

- Where do you see yourself in five years?

Don't, however, go in with your answers so prepared that they sound like robotic, knee-jerk responses. Rehearse them in a way that they'll actually sound unrehearsed and off-the-cuff.

You haven't performed in a play in over a year and they ask what you've done lately? Don't lie, but do embellish a little. Reply, "I recently did such-and-such." They don't have to know how recent "recently" is.

The interviewer will likely ask to see your picture and resume, so be sure to bring some with you. Be well versed with what is on it. Point out anything you feel may be interesting or vital for that person to know. He or she may want to discuss directors or work you've listed. No matter how unhappy the experience may have been, no matter how much you dislike the director in question, find pleasant things to say. Even if the interviewer waxes unkind about an individual or play, stay positive a la, "That may be true, but I had a great time." The key to giving a good interview is to keep upbeat, positive and to present yourself as a winner. Your primary goal in the interview is to effortlessly (at least ostensibly) seduce the person you're meeting with into wanting to work with you.

What Should I Talk About?

Agents, casting people, directors and producers want to work with well-rounded individuals, not job-hungry actors. Therefore, don't dominate the conversation talking only about your career or what you want. Discuss other aspects of your life like interests, hobbies, new experiences or wacky life stories (we all have them). Keep this positive and upbeat as well; industry people don't want to know about your unhappy childhood, breakup with your boyfriend or recent surgery. Save those stories for when you have established a relationship with that person.

Moreover, engage the person you're interviewing with in a conversation about himself or herself. Are they married? Do they have kids? Originally from New York? How did they get into "the business"? Listen carefully and show an interest in them as people, not just as a means to employment and stardom. Everyone likes to tell their story; you'll leave a good impression if you can get the person you're interviewing with to talk about him or herself.

Don't Panic

Some think that smoking and shopping are what separate us from the lower life forms. I think it's the interview panic attack. It's only human that, in any kind of interview in which our future is at stake (job interview, college admission, first date, etc.), we "leave our bodies" and our nerves take over, causing us to shake, stutter, and say really stupid things ("nice nylons"). If you're nervous in an interview, there are a couple of things you can do to calm yourself. First, take several deep breaths; this will center you and give you vamp time to think up appropriate answers to the questions you'll be asked. If you're still nervous, do the old trick of imagining that the interviewer is sitting there in his or her underwear, or in nothing at all. It's a way to make them more human to you, thus less desperately important, and it quells our run-amok nerves.

Don't Forget It's a Business Meeting

Several years ago, an actress friend met with the director of casting at a major television network, whom, for discretion's sake, I'll call "Sam." The interview was going swimmingly. My friend felt relaxed and comfortable and the casting director seemed genuinely interested in her. The atmosphere was jovial and they were trading stories and jokes, laughing and having a good time. The interview lasted nearly thirty minutes. Toward the end of the meeting, the actress, feeling like she had established a rapport with Sam, made a slightly teasing joke, as someone might do with a friend. Sam instantly stopped smiling; the mood immediately changed. My friend had clearly overstepped Sam's boundaries, was quickly shown the door and to this day, has never been in to audition for him. The moral? You can be friendly, but it's *always* a business meeting. Don't get too familiar.

Don't Overstay Your Welcome

Once all your questions have been answered and it's clear the interviewer has nothing more to discuss, thank that person for taking the time to meet with you, give a firm handshake and say goodbye. If it's an agent you're meeting with, ask if he or she'd like some pictures and resumes (that's why it's a good idea to always tote a stack of at least twenty with you to every interview) and what the next step might be. Whatever you do, don't linger longer than is necessary. Less is more in acting and in interviews!

Following Up

Always follow up your interview with a Thank You note. Keep the message sincere, warm and gracious, as well as short and sweet (no more than three lines are necessary). Picture postcards are ideal, as they will remind those that you met with who you are.

Interview Checklist

☑ Do your homework—research the person/office you'll be meeting with.

☑ Practice all aspects of the interview—how you enter and exit the room, how you sit, how you conduct yourself, etc.

☑ Have answers prepared to questions you're sure to be asked.

☑ Give a firm but friendly handshake at the beginning and end of the interview to the person you're interviewing with.

☑ Maintain eye contact—if you continually look away, you'll come off shy, secretive or unconfident.

☑ Don't forget your picture and resume.

☑ Know your resume inside and out so that you can point out anything that might be significant or interesting to the interviewer.

☑ Really listen to what the interviewer has to say.

☑ Don't get too personal about yourself or the interviewer—know your boundaries.

☑ Keep the interview positive, upbeat, enthusiastic.

☑ Don't dominate the conversation by talking only about your career—prepare to tell a funny anecdote or to talk about aspects of your life that have nothing to do with "the business."

☑ Ask the interviewers questions about themselves. Don't only talk about what they can or might do for you.

☑ Refrain from saying anything negative about people you've worked with or about bad past experiences. This business is too small and you'll never stop being amazed at who knows whom.

☑ Utilize breathing and creative visualization techniques during the interview to allay nerves and help you relax.

☑ Don't ever forget it's a business meeting.

☑ Know when to leave.

Personal
Presentation

As in life, instant assessments are made about us the minute we step into an office or audition room. How we present ourselves greatly influences the industry's desire to work with us and how we are "typed." Some would say pigeonholed. (For a full discussion on "type," its importance on our careers and how to determine what it is and how to develop it, see the "Take Control" chapter.) Part of our job is to leave a good impression on those who may be hiring us. No matter whether you are interviewing with an agent, lunching with a producer or auditioning for a Broadway show, there are rules you should follow about how to present yourself to "the business."

Hygiene

First, go looking clean. Clean face, clean hair, clean skin, clean nails, clean clothes. There's no bigger turn-off for auditors than to have to look at, shake hands with or smell a dirty actor. Unless you are auditioning for a homeless person or Cro-Magnon man (and even then, go clean and *suggest* the character by what you wear), going unkempt will send the implied message that you have no respect for yourself and no respect for the people you are auditioning for. Who would want to hire anyone who exhibits so little esteem for him or herself?

Hair, Face and Body

Do you have acne? Use Clearasil. Have a mono-brow? Wax it. Have a mouth of tobacco-tinged teeth? Bleach them. Do you need to lose a few pounds? Lose them. Gray hairs are coming in and you're still playing (or want to play) leading roles? Dye them. Dandruff? Get a bottle of Selsun Blue. To get ahead in this business, to surpass the competition and make an impression, we must always put our best foot forward. We need to exude confidence, control, discipline and style. Therefore, make sure that you are impeccably groomed. Get a haircut that suits your face, is stylish, and typical of your type. Join a gym and work out. If you're a woman and don't know how to apply makeup, take a class or get a free makeover in the cosmetic section of any department store.

What to Wear—Interviews

When meeting with agents, you need to look hip, cool, calm, collected, sexy, warm, personable and friendly. You have to walk in looking like you've got your act together, you have a sense of style, you're a success, that you will make money for yourself, and most importantly, for them. What you wear can't help but contribute to how you are perceived by the industry. What should you wear? That which will exhibit all the above and reflect and enhance what you are, what your type is. Go out and spend some money.

Don't have any fashion sense? Love to mix plaids? There's a great, *free* service to the rescue. **Macy's Department Store** (151 West 34th Street between Sixth and Seventh Avenues—212-494-4181) offers its **"Macy's By Appointment"** free personal shopper service that will pull together several ideas based on what you tell them you're looking for and on your budget. Call Macy's to set up an appointment. On the phone tell them your needs, sizes, skin tones, preferred colors and the statement you'd like to make with your clothes. At your appointment, they

GREAT
FREE
RESOURCE

will have pulled together several coordinated outfits for your perusal. (Note: This service is complimentary, but of course you will have to pay for the clothes.)

What to Wear—Auditions

What I said above about clothes for interviews holds true for auditions as well. But beyond this, in your audition you may want to suggest the essence of your character by what you wear. Whatever you do, don't go in looking like you're going to a costume party—you'll just appear hungry—that is, unless you're auditioning for a commercial where it's acceptable to go dressed as the businessman, nurse, young mom, waitress, or trailer park habitué you've been called in for. If auditioning for a Victorian play, women may want to wear a dress, men a suit, to suggest the period. If you're auditioning for a play's antagonist, you may want to wear dark clothes that suggest "bad guy" (or "bad gal"). If you're reading for a hooker, you may not want to wear Laura Ashley. If auditioning for a priest, you may not want to go in gym clothes. By what you wear, you can help the auditors imagine you in the role. Just remember, don't do all their work and go whole hog; it'll smack of desperation, and desperate actors are rarely cast.

If you are called back for something, no matter whether it is for theater, film, television or commercial work, go wearing exactly what you had on at the initial audition. Keep your hair the same way too. The casting director and the show's director called you back, so they liked the entire package you presented—acting and outward appearance. Give them what they like. By wearing the same outfit, you help them remember your first audition.

Whatever you wear, make sure that it is comfortable and allows you to move freely. It wouldn't hurt if your clothes also make you feel attractive, sexy, even "hot." This is a visual medium, after all, and often it's as much about the external package as it is about talent. If you feel like you look good, your confidence will be amplified. Depending on budget constraints, try to pull together a handful of audition/interview outfits intended to be worn strictly for those purposes. That way they're not overworn and overlaundered, and they stay crisp and fresh. Make sure they are clean, ironed and have no holes.

Finally, an anecdote I often tell that has to do with a suit: Over dinner one evening, my agent Nancy suggested that I buy an expensive, well-tailored suit. She told me, "You're coming into an age where you can play lots of businessmen and lawyers on TV. Go in looking the part and you'll get the job. But don't buy just any suit. Get one that looks like you spent a million bucks, that people will notice and will say, 'Jeez, that guy must work a lot; how else could he afford that suit?' "

I looked at her as if she had lost her mind, but the following weekend I went out and did major damage to my credit card. A week or so later I had an audition as a lawyer for a locally shot cop and justice show. I booked the role. When the casting director called my agent with details of the shoot, she asked if I could please bring the suit. I've done several appearances on the show, and although I have only worn the suit on the show once, every time they call looking for me, they say, "We want the suit!" I'm here to tell you it was the best investment of my career and has paid for itself several times over.

Showcases

What Is a Showcase?

A showcase is the presentation of a play or series of one-acts or scenes to showcase the talents of theater artists to potential future employers and to those who can help them find work. Of course, friends, family and anyone else may attend, but the showcase's primary purpose is to present the work of actors, directors, playwrights and designers to people in the industry. Showcases are usually produced in small (ninety-nine seats or less), funky, out-of-the-way venues (where rents are lower), and they are usually done on the cheap. Production values are minimal; actors are rarely paid other than subway fare ($4 per day); and it isn't unheard of for performers to provide their own costumes and props.

A showcase can benefit actors, especially those unknown who are just starting their New York careers. It's a way for agents, producers, casting directors and directors to see if you've got the goods and if they want to work with you. Finding an agent in the city is as hard as finding an apartment, and every actor has heard that abominable phrase, "Let me know when you're in something." A showcase is the "something."

More and more, showcases are becoming as prolific a presence in the city as are the Gap and Starbucks stores, which is good news for actors...the more showcases there are, the more actors are needed. Every week in *Backstage* and *Show Business Weekly*, you will find myriad casting notices for these productions. But, proceed with caution: Remember, a showcase is an opportunity to showcase YOU and to flex your acting muscles. Because there are so many showcases, and so many bad ones, industry people stay away unless the buzz is good or the theater or people involved are reputable. Before doing a showcase, do your research—always ask friends and agents what they've heard about the producing group, theater, director, etc.

The questions you should always ask yourself when doing a showcase are: Is this a play that industry people will want to see? Is it being done at a venue where people will come? Will the role adequately "showcase" me? How is the talent of the other performers? Who is directing? Will the play be publicized?

The best way to determine whether or not you want to do a particular showcase is to decide if it satisfies the "Eight Ps."

The "Eight Ps"

Several years ago I was weighing the pros and cons of accepting an offer I just received with my agent. "What should I do?" I whined. (Yeah, I can whine on occasion.)

"Well," she said, "do what I tell all my clients: Decide whether or not it passes the 'Six Ps' test."

"Huh?" I replied, not having a clue.

"The Six Ps—people, place, play, part, pay and production. If you respond positively to all six, accept it. If not, don't do it."

Great advice. I've used this rule with every job offer ever since, and have even added a couple of Ps to the list. It is an ideal barometer for gauging whether a particular showcase, or *any production* for that matter, is worth doing. Simply put, I ask myself if the production will satisfy the following:

1. **P**lay—Am I passionate about the play? Is it something I'm burning to do?

2. **P**lace—Is it being produced in a place where I (and those whom I invite to see the play) will be comfortable? Is it a place where I will want to spend a lengthy amount of time?

3. **P**art—Is it a role I want to work on?

4. **P**eople—Do I want to collaborate with these people, this theater?

5. **P**roduction—How are the production values? Will the production be compelling to an audience? Will it be embarrassing or harmful to my career to be a part of this production?

6. **P**roducers—Are the people who are producing this play reputable? Do they have a good track record? Is there any bad buzz about them?

7. **P**ay—Will it be financially remunerative? By doing this production, will I be ahead or behind financially (of course, in the case of a showcase, there is almost never any pay other than subway fare).

8. **P**ublicity—Will there be any press for this project? Will the show be reviewed?

(Note: There is no reason to do a showcase if it is *not* going to bring you joy, help you grow as an artist and attract theater professionals that can help you.)

The Equity Approved Showcase

If you are a member of Actors' Equity, you may only perform in an Equity approved showcase. Don't even think about flouting this rule, as there are financial and other consequences if you are caught, and *you will be caught*. (However, if you are non-union, you are allowed to perform in an Equity showcase.) An AEA showcase must conform to a series of rules and protections (known as the Showcase Code), including:

● The total budget of a showcase may not exceed $15,000.

● A showcase producer may schedule up to twelve perform- ances of a Showcase Code production within a four-week pe- riod. An additional four performances may be added at $10 per show per Equity actor.

● An Equity member is due reimbursement payments of no less than minimum public transportation costs ($4 per day) for all rehearsals and performances of a showcase production.

● Complimentary tickets must be made available to industry people (agents, directors, casting people, producers, etc.).

● There is a proscribed maximum price per ticket that a theater may charge.

● Since actors and stage managers are not paid under the Show- case Code and do not receive the same benefits and protections of a standard agreement, there is no obligation to remain in a showcase production. Moreover, all AEA members may view these shows at no cost.

● The actor is guaranteed future rights or must be compensated should the protection move to a standard agreement.

● All rehearsals are subject to the actor's availability.

● The maximum rehearsal period is four consecutive weeks and the rehearsals on a given day may not exceed six hours, with a day off after six consecutive rehearsal days. Three eight-hour days may be scheduled the final week of rehearsal.

- The standard Off-Broadway rehearsal breaks apply.

- The Showcase Code is an agreement, not a contract, and members participate without benefit of salary or pension and health.

- If you are an Equity member and you think you are participating in a Showcase Code production that has not been filed with AEA or not been approved, call the Showcase Department at 212-869-8530.

Unions

Once upon a time in our fair country's not too distant past, actors, like most other workers, were an oppressed lot. They were paid little or no money and made to work inhumanly long hours in unsafe and unsavory environments. Finally, in 1919, actors rebelled against exploitative producers and directors by establishing the Actors' Equity Association (AEA or "Equity"), the first of several performing artist unions. Today, through collective bargaining agreements with producers, actors' unions protect their membership in several ways: they guarantee their members minimum salaries, health and retirement benefits, safe and clean working conditions, and a finite number of hours they are allowed to work each day (if work goes beyond the proscribed number of hours, producers must now compensate actors by paying overtime). Unions also look after their members by, among other things:

- Forcing producers to post bonds guaranteeing salaries and benefits if a project goes bust.

- Providing legal counseling.

- Maintaining bulletin boards listing member services, classified ads for items for sale and apartment rentals and sublets, casting notices and obituaries.

- Trouble-shooting problems between producers and members.

- Offering financial assistance to members in need.

- Qualifying members for credit union membership.

- Setting up guidelines for how agents may treat actors and agent commission payments.

We've come a long way, and unions have contributed much to making our work safe, comfortable and remunerative.

To Join or Not to Join, That Is the Question

Is it your hope to be a Broadway, film or TV star? Do you see yourself acting in an off-Broadway play, at one of the several regional theaters around the country or in a commercial and/or voice-over (which is the voice of an unseen actor heard during a scene or shot, used for narration, commentary or to regale the virtues of a product being showcased in a commercial)? Do you want to make a living wage plying your craft? If you answered yes to any of these, you should seriously consider eventually joining a performing artist union. As most major theater, film, television and advertising producers are union signatories (meaning that they have signed agreements with the unions pledging to employ union members), if you want to work for them, you'll have to be a union member.

Before joining a union you should ask yourself, "Am I ready?" If you are just beginning your acting career, you may want to hold off. Joining a union will keep you from doing non-union work, which is one of the best training grounds for actors just starting out. In the beginning of your career, you'll probably want to get as much experience as you can, which is easier to do in the more numerous non-union productions.

Once you feel like you've gotten enough non-union work under your belt, you've "paid your dues" (as you literally will, since most of this work pays little or nothing) and you're ready to compete for professional work, you'll want to join a union. In becoming a union member, there are a couple of caveats. First, once a union member, you may never again work in non-union productions; if you do, you risk being fined, and in some cases, having your membership revoked. Second, the cost of joining a union is expensive (an initial fee of $1,000 for AEA, $1,406 for SAG, $1,360 for AFTRA—start saving your money now), after which you are also required to pay annual dues, calculated as a percentage of your earnings as an actor.

The Three Main Performing Arts Unions

Although the list of performing artist unions in the New York area is a long one (see "Index of Actor Resources and Services"), the three that most actors need to know about and ultimately join are:

1. Actors' Equity Association (AEA)

Actors' Equity Association (165 West 46th Street, 14th Floor, New York, NY, 10036—212-869-8530, www.actorsequity.org), the oldest of the performing artist unions, oversees actors who work in theater. For membership eligibility, you must meet one of three requirements:

- Secure work under an Equity standard contract in a union sanctioned production.

- Work fifty weeks as an "Equity Membership Candidate" in union-sanctioned productions/theaters. Several theaters throughout the country employ this program in which non-union actors, in exchange for working fifty weeks, are eligible to join AEA (the weeks don't have to be consecutive). Also, you may join AEA after working 40 weeks as a membership candidate if you're willing to take a test on Equity rules. (Don't sweat it, though—it's a take-home exam and you're allowed to refer to the rule book.)

● Provide proof that you have been a paid-up member in good standing of another performing union such as AFTRA or SAG for at least one year and worked a certain number of weeks or earned a minimum amount of money under either's jurisdiction.

Annual dues are $118, paid half in May, half in November. Also, two percent of your Equity earnings up to $150,000 are assessed as working dues, deducted from your paycheck and forwarded to AEA by your producer/employer. (Note: All union dues, initiation fees and assessments are tax deductible.)

2. American Federation of Television and Radio Artists (AFTRA)

The American Federation of Television and Radio Artists (260 Madison Avenue, 7th Floor, New York, NY 10016—212-532-0800, www.aftra.org) covers performers and broadcasters in television, radio and sound recordings, including entertainment, industrial, interactive and educational programming and CD-ROMs. Since both AFTRA and SAG protect television actors, what each covers is differentiated this way: If a show is shot on videotape (e.g., soap operas, reality shows, game shows, news programs), it comes under AFTRA's jurisdiction; if shot on film (commercials, sitcoms, serials), it comes under SAG's.

AFTRA is an open union, meaning anyone who wishes to may join; all you have to do is pony up the initiation fee. Dues, which are based on your previous year's union income, are paid semiannually (May and November); if you have had no AFTRA earnings in a previous year, your dues will be assessed at a flat rate fee.

3. Screen Actors Guild (SAG)

The Screen Actors Guild (360 Madison Avenue, 12th Floor, New York, NY 10036—212-944-1030, www.sag.org) oversees film, industrials, commercials, rock videos and some television programming. (See the discussion about AFTRA above for how this breaks down.) To be eligible for membership, you must satisfy one of the following:

- Join through the Taft-Hartley Act clause, which allows non-union members to work up to 30 days on a union production. At the end of that time, you must join SAG if you wish to continue doing union work.

- Provide proof of employment (contract, check stub, paycheck, production company letter on letterhead) or of prospective employment as a principal or speaking role in a SAG signatory project.

- Show that you have been a paid-up member in good standing of another performing union such as AEA or AFTRA for at least one year and have had a principal role under either union's jurisdiction.

- Provide proof that you worked at least three days as an extra on a SAG film or commercial for which you were compensated at union scale.

The formula for SAG dues is thus: In addition to being billed $50 twice a year (to be paid in May and November), you are assessed 1.85 percent of your SAG income up to $200,000; 0.5 percent between $200,000 and $500,000. SAG will assess your earnings and bill you bi-annually (May and November).

(Note: For more information about a particular union's membership eligibility requirements, contact the union office in question. Once you have become a member of a performing union, your employers must be union signatories and your agents must be union franchised. If you have any questions or concerns about this, contact the respective office before signing a contract.)

Demo Reels and
Working on Film

Demo Reels

A demo reel is a VHS or DVD copy of snippets of the best moments of an actor's work in student, independent, workshop and feature films, TV shows, soaps, commercials, industrials and music videos. The length of an actor's reel may vary from two to twelve minutes, with most industry people agreeing that three to five is best (less is more!). The point of the reel is to showcase your talent, type and range to agents, casting people, film and TV directors, producers, network executives, and anyone else who can help you get work as an actor.

The demo reel, which not so very long ago was almost solely used by actors pursuing work in L.A., is becoming more and more important as a marketing tool here in the Big Apple. It helps an agent, who may be interested in signing you, to see your work. It helps a casting director who can't imagine you in certain roles to see you in a different light. The purpose of the reel is to show the powers that be that you can in fact act.

The most effective reels open with a title of the actor's name, then either a photo or montage of images of him or her in various roles, usually with music playing underneath. This is followed by a series of clips of the actor's best moments in a wide range of roles and actions. Often they include titles ("NYPD Blue," "Law & Order," "Sex and the City," etc.) to identify each clip. Most reels end with a still photograph of the actor and contact information. The reel is the video equivalent of a picture and resume, and like these, should be updated periodically with new work. When creating and editing your demo reel, don't cut corners by using someone with little or no experience. Like I warned against earlier about your headshot, by doing your demo on the cheap, you may get exactly what you paid for. A professionally produced reel is an investment in your career and future, and may be written off on your taxes. (For a list of demo reel editors, see the "Index of Actor Resources and Services" section.)

(Note: Keep nudity out of the clip, and if there is a kiss or physical intimacy, show just a hint of it and fade to black. Do not feature background ("extra") work; although you've done it to pay the bills, to make connections and get valuable experience working on film, extra work is not acting and you never want industry people to see you as less than the unique and talented actor you are. Also, do not include clips of stage work. Although you may have been the definitive Hamlet, Mary Tyrone or Little Buttercup, stage work, which was not created or blocked for the camera, almost never translates well to film.)

About now you may be thinking, "That's all well and good, but I've never done any film or television work. How can I put together a reel if I have nothing to contribute to it?" Read on...

Student and Independent Films

By the time you have arrived in New York to fulfill your dreams, you have, hopefully, honed your skills for the stage. You have worked on using your imaginative faculties; you've created your own system of delving into a play's given circumstances; you know how to build a character. You have trained your voice and speech, learned to access your inner life and mastered scene analysis skills. You know how to make an entrance and an exit, you know when you may (and may not) pull focus, and you can actually navigate a set without bumping into the furniture. You are ready to work on the stage. You feel at home in a theater.

What's that you say? You want to win a Tony AND an Oscar?

How do you do that when all your training has been for the stage? How do you translate your stage technique to acting on the big screen? How can you get auditions for work in film or television if you've never had experience in either medium (the great Catch-22 of the biz)?

The answer: the same way you developed your skills for the stage—PRACTICE! Enrolling in a class is of course very important. There is however no better training than the hands-on, practical experience of working in front of a camera. In order to gain this experience, you must actually be in as many movies as possible. How? Get yourself into student, independent and workshop films.

Student films are those made by, you guessed it, film school students; independent films are fashioned by auteurs working outside the Hollywood system. They are usually low- to no-budget endeavors, where a lot of the crew are getting on-the-job training and novices (or even members of the filmmaker's family) are in key positions like set designer or boom microphone operator. Actors are almost never paid other than for travel, food and lodging. Most often these films don't have a run outside of private screenings for the teachers, friends and family of those involved on the film. There is the occasional Cinderella story where a student film or "indie" gets recognition at film festivals, wins awards and goes on to be a blockbuster, but this is definitely the exception to the rule. It is more likely that most of these are never finished, or take months, even years of maxing out credit cards, pursuing donated services and illicitly "borrowing" equipment to complete. The appeal of these films for actors, besides the experience of working in front of a camera, is that if the film comes to fruition, a copy of the completed project is available to add to a demo reel.

How can you get work on these films? Open a copy of *Backstage* or *Show Business Weekly* any given week and you'll find countless casting notices for these projects.

Workshop Films

The Workshop film is another avenue for actors looking to perfect their film technique and compile material for their demo reels. The workshop film is a character-driven "mini movie" (usually about fifteen minutes long), shot on digital video. The production values are simple yet professional, and the actor's performance is the centerpiece of the film. This film is a hybrid of the off-off-Broadway showcase (actors are responsible for costumes and props) and a film acting class (hence the "workshop" designation). Although there is a fee to participate in a workshop film, it is usually scripted for the unique talents of the actors involved and is first-rate (more often than not those viewing a clip from a workshop film in an actor's reel have no idea that the actor paid to be a part of it). For those who have had no film experience, the workshop film is a great means for actors to play original supporting and leading film roles, while at the same time creating material for their reels.

Several city acting studios and production companies offer workshop film courses to actors. One company, **Red Wall Productions** (400 West 43rd Street, Suite 10L, New York, NY, 10036—212-695-6669, www.redwallproductions.com), is creating some of the best films of this genre in the industry. Red Wall's founders, Craig and Rosalyn Coleman-Williams, are actors-turned-impassioned-filmmakers who understand the needs of actors. They write meaty, compelling stories for the specific talents of the actors in each of their films, and coach them throughout the shoot to elicit their best work. At the end of the year, they ask industry professionals to judge the work of the actors appearing in their films and hold an annual awards night in which they present best supporting and leading acting awards. As a special offer to readers of *An Actor Prepares ... To Work in New York City,* Red Wall is offering a ten percent

SPECIAL OFFER

discount on its workshop film services. For more information, contact them at the number above.

Demo Reel Checklist

For a top-quality reel, try incorporating the following:

☑ Begin with your name and either a headshot or a montage of images of you in various roles. Music playing beneath this introduction makes the reel more compelling.

☑ Select scenes that feature you in a variety of roles and actions; show range, nuance, versatility, and subtlety.

☑ Use titles to announce which television show or film the scene appeared in.

☑ End with a photo, your name again and contact information.

☑ Try not to go longer than five minutes—remember, less is more.

☑ Periodically update your reel.

☑ Use a tried-and-true professional demo reel editor. By doing it on the cheap, you'll get exactly what you pay for.

☑ Make sure that the master tape you give the reel editor is of good quality.

☑ Key the master tapes up to your scenes before giving them to the editor. Too much studio time is wasted trying to locate scenes, and time is money—your money.

☑ Put your name, address and contact information on the video box and jacket. Avery makes a great label (#5997—available at most office supply stores) that is easy to format to create custom videotape labels that can incorporate your information, graphics, even your headshot.

☑ Make the demo reel as engaging as possible. Casting directors, agents, producers, network executives and directors see thousands of these things—you want yours to stand out.

Avoid Getting
Sucker-Punched

As in most fields of human endeavor, there are those few in our business whose incomes are derived from taking advantage of naïve naïfs. These morally bankrupt opportunists prey on and exploit the ignorance of vulnerable but ambitious actors newly arrived in the Big Apple by flattery and assurances of stardom, fame and fortune. Intoxicated by the promise of success, unsuspecting actors give their money, trust and dreams to these con artists who deliver nothing more than broken hearts and raided savings accounts.

How do you avoid becoming a victim of these scammers and con artists? Keep your eyes open and maintain a robust, cautious skepticism. The maxim, "If it sounds too good to be true, it probably is," is especially applicable in our profession. If you are at all suspicious of an industry person's intentions, heed the following: If a "producer," "casting director," "agent," "manager," "director," or other "industry" person (the quotation marks are intentional) guarantees overnight success, be wary. (The *only* guarantee in this business is that there are no guarantees.) If someone asks for a fee to meet with you, represent you or provide you with work, they are in violation of union rules and labor laws and should be avoided. No matter how much you enjoy having your ego stroked, no matter how much you like being told that you're the next big thing, any time you have to pay someone in order to be "discovered" or to get ahead, you can be assured you won't achieve either.

Scams and Con Artists to Avoid

- Any meeting with or audition for an agent, casting director, producer, manager or director in which you are asked to pay a fee or give any kind of compensation for being seen.

- An audition situation in which you are required to pay to present a scene or monologue to someone who claims to be looking for actors for current or future projects; this is in essence a paid audition. There are legitimate "Meet the Pros" seminars and workshops (for a description of these, see the "Agents" and "Casting Directors" chapters) with industry people in which a fee is required; the difference between these and a paid audition is that in the latter your work is usually critiqued (and possibly tweaked) and you are never told that the purpose of the seminar or workshop is to discover talent.

- An audition for which you are asked to pay a "registration" or "application" fee.

- Film producers or production companies and theatrical groups that offer a role to anyone (regardless of talent and/or experience) in exchange for contributing money toward the financing of the film or play.

- Agents and managers who railroad you into having your headshot done (for which you will have to pay) only by their recommended photographer. Odds are you'll spend much more money than if you found a photographer on your own (after all, the photographer is no doubt giving the referring agent or manager a sizable kickback) and the shots will be crummy. A legitimate agency almost always provides clients with a list of *several* photographers for you to choose from whose work they know and like.

- Industry people who claim they can help you get ahead as long as you take their class (for which you have to pay a fee) as a prerequisite for working with them.

- Any agent or manager who requests a commission in advance. The union rules are very clear about this: you are required to pay a commission only *after* you've been paid.

- Anyone who refuses to enter into a contract or written agreement with you. If you are told, "Trust me" or "We don't need a contract," head for the hills.

- Anyone who claims that an opportunity has opened up for you (e.g., a class, seminar, workshop, job, meeting, audition, etc.) if you proceed immediately into a financial transaction with them (in which money goes from your wallet into their hands) without time to do your research or weigh whether or not you want to participate.

- Any agent or manager who requires a deposit or fee (separate from a commission) to represent you.

- Agents and managers who insist you pay them for additional publicity materials like postcards, brochures, or inclusion in the agency's "book," "client sheet" (a poster of client headshots) or on its website. Inclusion in these is a waste of your money, as no one will see them; they are fashioned solely to generate income for these charlatans. The *legitimate* books you may want to consider placing your headshot, resume and biographical information in are, as I've already said, the *Academy Players Directory* and the *Players' Guide New York* (see the "Directories" section of the "Index of Actor Resources and Services" or the "Mailings and Marketing" chapter).

* Agents or managers who pressure you to take classes with one particular teacher. Any agent worth his or her salt knows that no teacher is right for every actor; if someone steers you to one and only one teacher, you can be sure that they are receiving a kickback.

* Casting calls and agent notices that state "No experience necessary." Proceed with trepidation.

* Any acting teacher who *guarantees* stardom and worldwide household name status if only you'll study with him or her (and of course pay for the honor of being in his or her class).

* Any industry person who asks you to do anything untoward (remove your clothes, trade sex for a role). As I said earlier, if you are auditioning for a legitimate play in which nudity is required, you will be given notice in advance (and usually asked to undress down to a bathing suit only), and there is often a union representative present to monitor the audition.

If you are at all doubtful about the legitimacy of an industry person, office or organization, there are several ways you can verify their authenticity and reputation:

* Ask actors and others in the business what they've heard about the agent, manager, director, casting person or producer in question; in our business, word travels fast, as well as bad reputations.

● No matter whether you are a member of a performing union or not, you may consult them (see the chapter on "Unions") to determine if an agent or casting person is associated with or franchised by the union and considered to be in good standing. Moreover, if you are a union member and suspect that you are being swindled, contact your union office immediately to report the incident.

● Check the **Ross Reports** (see the "Periodicals and Theater Related Publications" section of the "Index of Actor Resources and Services") to see if they are listed.

● If doubtful as to the veracity of a casting person or agency, contact the **Casting Society of America (CSA)** (www.castingsociety.com); to learn more about an agent, contact the **National Association of Talent Representatives** (315 West 57th Street, New York, NY 10019—212-262-5696, www.agentassociation.com).

● Call the **Better Business Bureau** (257 Park Avenue South, New York, NY 10010—212-533-6200, www.newyork.bbb.org) and inquire if any complaints have been lodged about the person or people in question.

● The **Department of Consumer Affairs** (42 Broadway, New York, NY 10004—800-275-8777) is a good source to consult, as it keeps a database of con artists and scams that have been filed by duped actors.

Respect

In our overcrowded field, it is well nigh impossible to get seen, become known, and, most importantly, gain respect from the powers that may employ us or help us find work. It's a daily struggle that we all have to wage if we're going to make it in this profession. Many of the things I've already discussed—having a killer headshot, marketing yourself, creating an attention-grabbing resume, knowing the audition fundamentals, having a good understanding of how the business works, honing your craft, etc.—will do much to help you get seen and known in the industry. Respect however is a more nebulous, more esoteric thing. You can't touch or hold respect like you can a picture or a resume. Respect isn't something you can acquire by taking a class. Respect is achieved by the way you live your life, treat yourself and others, and conduct yourself in the business. To gain respect, you must show respect.

Below are some thoughts I have about the ways to be respectful in order to not only command respect, but to also be a better artist, a better member of the performing community, and a better member of the world at large.

To garner respect, you should value:

Yourself—Be mindful of your appearance and your health. Work out frequently. Bathe every day. Brush your teeth often and floss at least once a day. Try to get seven to eight hours of sleep a night. Take naps when you can. Eat healthfully. If you're overweight, diet. If you're too thin (you know who you are, Calista), eat something. If you smoke, drink or use drugs (no value judgment here), do them in moderation. Sex is a great thing—have as much as you want, with whomever you want, anytime, anywhere, but for your health's sake, use protection. If you need therapy, get it. If you don't feel well, see a doctor. Respect your mind: read, partake of all the arts, and attend classes on subjects that interest you. The bottom line is, you are your instrument. Like a violinist who plays a Stradivarius, treat your instrument with care so that it looks great, is at peak performance and lasts a long, long time.

Your craft—Take an acting- or performance-related class to enhance your skills or to learn new ones. Attend theater and watch films and television to study the work of other actors. While caught up in the maelstrom of trying to master the business of "the business," don't forget that you are first and foremost an artist. As Stanislavski said, "Love the art in you, not you in the art." Moreover, just because many dismiss what we do as being trivial, vain or unimportant, don't you do it too; never apologize for being an artist ("I'm *just* an actor").

The industry—When meeting, interviewing with or auditioning for directors, casting directors, producers and agents, be warm, courteous and friendly. Say "hello" and "thank you." Don't pander or be sycophantic, but also don't be cold, distant or aloof. Send a Thank You note to a casting director if he or she has cast you in a show. Send holiday cards to all the members of the industry you know. Don't be demanding or rude with your agents and do remember them at Christmas or Hanukah (gifts to the industry up to $25 per person are tax-deductible). Finally, be careful about what you say about people in the industry and whom you say it to. "The business" is really tiny and backbiting has a nasty way of getting back to the back that's been bitten.

Theater professionals—One of an actor's favorite pastimes is to assess the work of other performing artists. Often that scrutiny can get downright nasty. To put a positive spin on this, one could say that it's because we're passionate about what we do; we care. It would be hypocritical of me to tell you not to trash the work of others; I'm effusive about great work but have been known on more than one occasion to rant vociferously when work is bad. What you should be respectful of is when and where you do it. Express your opinions freely, but be discreet. If you're at the theater and hate what you've seen, save your opinions until you get home or to a bar or restaurant. Those sitting in the audience around you might have loved the performance; your negative comments will ruin it for them. Likewise, you never know who's sitting in the seat next to, in front of, or behind you . . . the mother of the star, the husband of the ingénue, the boyfriend of the director. Put yourself in their place. Would you want someone to loudly trash a loved one of yours for everyone in a theater to hear? Would you want them to do that about you? Do unto others . . . . Moreover, it could be the director, producer or casting person sitting nearby who hears your unflattering comments. Since no one in "the business" forgets a thing, you'll be remembered, and your chances of working with those people will be negligible.

Fellow actors—Not all acting experiences are positive ones. Often we're cast in projects in which an actor or actors is nasty, selfish, incapable of playing a role or giving us what we need to play our role, who upstage us or are just plain bad. All of these can really rankle. However, it is not our job to give our fellow actors notes, to inform them of their ineptitude or to exact revenge. If you have a problem with someone you're working with, go to the director, stage manager or producer to discuss your beefs. It's their job to remedy the problem. Moreover, don't disparage an actor you're working with to others. Whether you like it or not, you have to work with that person. No matter how unpleasant the situation is, you still have to show up and do your job. Grumbling about another will only intensify your anger and dislike, increase your blood pressure and ultimately influence your work. If you have a problem, go through the appropriate channels to have it resolved.

The work of artists in other fields—As tempting and easy as it is, don't steal the work of other artists. If you download music, pay for it. Don't buy pirated tapes of film and theatrical performances or illegally copied CDs. You want to be compensated for all of your work, right? Well, shouldn't other artists receive remuneration as well?

Your community—Our artistic medium can be healing. It can be inspiring. It can educate. It can please. It can create catharsis and hope. Actors, as Hamlet says, are "the abstract and brief chronicles of the time." That is a lot of responsibility, but as artists, we need to embrace it. In this, it is my belief that what we do is a service to the community. We are public servants. It is also my belief that in our private lives, we should serve the community in some capacity as well, whether by volunteering for charitable organizations, or donating goods, food or money to charities and those less fortunate than ourselves. Moreover, embrace your jury duty obligations, get involved in politics and by all means, vote.

The environment—Don't litter. Whenever possible, use environmentally friendly and biodegradable products. Be conscious and conscientious about the gas mileage of the vehicle you drive. Better yet, take public transportation. Recycle.

Take Control

As I have stated ad nauseam, to succeed in this very competitive business, you must take control of your career. You must mentor your career. The success (and failure) of your career is squarely on your shoulders. Nothing and no one—no agent, manager, casting person, director, producer, or stage mother—is going to make your career happen without your active, nay, proactive participation. Your success as an actor is wholly dependent on the energy, focus and drive you put into your career.

Besides what I've already covered in previous chapters, I offer the following tips, in no particular order, on practical ways for you to take control:

My formula for success is rise early, work late and strike oil.
—J. PAUL GETTY

As I've said several times, view your career as your corporation with you as the CEO, COO, CFO, president, chairman of the board, manager, employee, receptionist and general lackey. Therefore, work at your career like a CEO and all of his minions would work at maintaining and developing their company. That means, devote eight hours a day, five days a week to your career, your corporation. A full eight hours a day. A full five days a week. No, I haven't lost my mind. If you work in any other profession, you'd be doing this, and undoubtedly for someone else. You'd be doing it to help grow someone else's company. So, why not put that same effort into growing your own, which is, in essence, you? Moreover, if you owned your own business, you would no doubt work as hard as you could, as many hours as you could to make it a success. Why not dedicate that same effort to your acting career?

What does this entail exactly? Basically, anything you can think of that contributes to making you a better, more successful actor, and a better, more successful businessperson: acting classes, voice lessons, speech and elocution studies, dance and movement classes, auditions, preparing auditions, research, reading plays, play readings, mailings, reading trade papers and magazines, generating publicity announcements, rehearsing scenes and monologues, viewing theater and films, contacting industry people, schmoozing industry people, working out—you name it. At the end of each "business" day, my hope is that you will reflect back on that day's efforts with pride, knowing that you labored mightily to make your corporation thrive.

> *All work and no play makes Jack a dull boy.*
> —OVERUSED ADAGE

Having said that, don't be so single-minded in the pursuit of your career that you forget to have a life. We are so much more than just actors and, in the interest of our art, we need to be well-rounded, multifaceted human beings. Simply put, we can't be expected to play other people, create other lives, if we're not truly living. We need to be immersed in life if we're going to portray it. So, go out and live. Have fun. Date. Fall in love. Cultivate friendships. Read. Write. Exercise. Pick up hobbies. Make things. Pursue all your interests. Get involved in politics. Open a newspaper. Go dancing. Smell the proverbial roses. Be curious. Devour all the arts and culture you can consume. Take classes outside your chosen field. Take advantage of all the pleasures this amazing city has to offer. Busy yourself in the world. You'll be a better, more engaging person; you'll be a better, more engaging actor.

Obstacles are those frightful things you see when you take
your eyes off your goal.   —HENRY FORD

To keep your career focused and on track, set a series of goals for yourself. You should have both short-term goals (those you can achieve in a few days, weeks or months) and long-range aspirations (where you see yourself in a year, five years). Write them down so you don't forget them, and carry them with you at all times (mine are attached to the front of my appointment book). Keep them realistic and make sure they are organized and defined clearly. Refer to them constantly. Check them off as you achieve them. Continually add new objectives to the list. Don't limit them to simple things—go for broke, have big dreams and desires; the bigger they are the harder you'll strive to accomplish them. Include all aspects of your career ("I will meet so-and-so by next month," "I will send out twenty-five pictures and resumes a week," "I will land a guest-starring role on a TV show within the year") *and* your personal life ("I will find my own apartment within the next four months," "I will run six miles a day," "I will find a decent survival job by the end of the week"). The key to setting goals is that you not just pursue them but that you believe in them and have faith they can be achieved. If you "keep your eyes on the prize," the built-in obstacles of this business will dissolve until they become inconsequential.

I'm good enough, I'm smart enough, and dog-gonnit, people
like me.   —STUART SMALLY

When I arrived in New York City many moons ago, at the ripe age of 26, my first year in New York was pretty tough. I spent most of that year finding a home and an agent, making contacts and getting settled. I was, for the most part, employment-challenged. At the end of that year, when I went to have my tax returns done, my accountant looked at the previous year's wages, compared them to the years before when I was working at a theater in Washington, D.C. and asked, "What happened? You didn't have as good a year as you have had in the past." I explained that I'd spent most of that time getting settled, making connections, learning the ropes, blah, blah, blah. He asked, "Craig, when you're outside a room waiting to go in and audition, what do you think about?" I told him I thought about the role, the lines, my objectives, what I've been working on. He said, "That's all well and good, but let me give you a piece of advice, something that worked for me when I was an actor and has worked for everyone I've shared it with: Each time you go into an audition room, I want you to think one thought. That thought is: 'I am a star.' Keep repeating over and over to yourself, 'I am a star.' " I loved that. For my next audition and each subsequent audition, my mantra was and is "I am a star." For me, this psychological trick calms my nerves, centers me, and gives me a boost of confidence. Try it. Before you walk into a meeting with an agent or an audition, say to yourself, and MEAN IT, "I am a star." See if that doesn't make you feel more empowered and able to really sell yourself.

> *I don't know the key to success, but the key to failure is to try to please everyone.* —BILL COSBY

Your uniqueness is a good thing. Don't give people what you think they want—give them who *you* are. Present *yourself*. There's no one else like you; you are unique.

Know thyself.   —DIOGENES LAËRTIUS

Haven't a clue who you are? Or how others perceive you? You'd better figure it out. In this business, you have to know who you are, what you project and what your "type" is. This is how you are going to be marketing yourself: your headshot, audition pieces, even the way you dress for auditions and interviews should reflect and convey your type. Hate limiting yourself like this? Feel like you can play anything? Too bad. As in life, we are assessed almost instantly in this business and are put into categories. We have no control over this. Our job as actors is to discern what our type is and present that type to the best of our ability. Don't fight against your type; instead, play into it.

The best way to determine your type is to ask around. Friends, family, colleagues, classmates, agents, casting directors, directors and teachers will all have opinions as to how you come off. Not everyone will completely agree, but there will be a consensus. Also, ask yourself what roles you have played in the past. What kinds of things are you auditioning for now? What material has been assigned to you by acting teachers and coaches? The answers will give you a pretty good idea of your type.

Most games are lost, not won.   —CASEY STENGEL

For an actress to be a success she must have the face of Venus, the brains of Minerva, the grace of Terpsichore, the memory of Macaulay, the figure of Juno, and the hide of a rhinoceros.
                                                —ETHEL BARRYMORE

Develop a thick skin because there is no other business that re-

jects us more than our business. Get used to hearing the word
"No." Let "No" be your friend.

What helps luck is a habit of watching for opportunities.
                                        —CHARLES VICTOR CHERBULIEZ

Always, and I mean always, carry a few pictures and resumes
with you, no matter where you go. This big city is really very
small and you'll frequently bump into agents, producers, casting
people, directors and other actors who may be working on a project that you are right for. When opportunity knocks, open the
door and hand it a headshot and resume!

Never burn bridges. Today's junior prick, tomorrow's senior
partner.   —KEVIN WADE, *WORKING GIRL*

Of everyone who works in the business, who do you think are the
people we most need to be nice to? Who are the people we should
be fostering relationships with? If you answered "agents" or
"casting directors" or "directors" or "producers," you'd be partially correct—yes, of course, we must be nice, personable and
friendly to these important people. But, the folks most important
to our careers are...ASSISTANTS! That's right, the assistants to
agents, casting directors and producers are the people most important to our futures and livelihoods. Why? Today they are assistants, tomorrow, however, they may hold your career in the
balance. No assistant in this business sets out to be an assistant.
No secretary in this business sets out to be a secretary. In the soul
of an assistant lurks an agent, producer, director, or casting director ready to emerge. Be especially nice to them.

I find that the harder I work, the more luck I seem to have.
                                        —THOMAS JEFFERSON

Get yourself into as many projects, dubious or otherwise, as you possibly can. Readings, plays, workshops, showcases, student films—you name it. It's important to constantly flex your acting muscles while also making new connections. Connections beget work, and work begets more work.

Good afternoon, Mrs. Cleaver. What a lovely apron you're wearing.   —EDDIE HASKELL, *LEAVE IT TO BEAVER*

Never underestimate the power of sucking up to those who have the authority to provide you with employment. What kind of sucking up is acceptable? Almost any subtle thing, from schmoozing at a party or opening night (this is where, as one friend says, "the 'keep me in mind' horseshit really pays off"), to Thank You notes, holiday cards, flowers or gifts (up to $25 per person per year only if you want to write them off on your taxes), a cocktail or meal, theater tickets to see you in a show. Whatever you do, don't be transparent, don't be obsequious, and don't appear too "hungry."

Nothing is illegal if one hundred businessmen decide to do it.
                                        —ANDREW YOUNG

When I began writing this, I sent out a mass e-mailing to all of the actors in my database, asking for suggestions, stories and sound bites that might be pertinent to actors new to the city. One friend, an actor who's been around for a while and who's had his share of ups and downs, wrote the following:

" . . . pay some1 2 get those breakdowns! in this internet age, they're available to everyone, so when U find a connection, fork over those bucks & get those illegal things. self-submitting is considerably more effective w/bkdn. Information than thru other avenues."

For those of you who don't understand this particular e-speak patois, I'll translate (please don't misconstrue my inclusion of this as in any way condoning this suggestion; I am passing this on out of the necessity for full disclosure): Each weekday, Breakdown Services transmits to agents and managers via the internet, information about acting roles that are soon to be cast. These listings are called breakdowns and usually provide descriptions of character qualities and types of actors being sought. Agents and managers peruse them, determine who from their roster would be appropriate for each role and submit those actors to the corresponding casting director. As you may have guessed, these breakdowns are for the eyes of agents and managers only. What my friend (who shall remain nameless to protect the guilty) was suggesting is that you get ahold of the breakdowns to see what is being cast, and, if you don't have an agent, submit yourself. How do you get the breakdowns? Well, there is a network of resourceful actors out there who, to the displeasure of Breakdown Services, receive them covertly and pass them on for a price. I am, on average, asked about once or twice a month if I'd like to enter the "network" (as yet, I've refrained). As it's only a matter of time and connections before you'll be asked to, please keep in mind that receiving the breakdowns is technically illegal.

I remember about the fifth time I ever went on 'Wise Child.' Seymour'd told me to shine my shoes just as I was going out the door. I was furious. The studio audience were all morons,

the announcer was a moron, the sponsors were morons, and I
just damn well wasn't going to shine my shoes for them . . . .
He said to shine them anyway . . . for the Fat Lady. I didn't
know what the hell he was talking about . . . but I shined my
shoes for the Fat Lady every time . . . . This terribly clear, clear
picture of the Fat Lady formed in my mind. I had her sitting
on this porch all day, swatting flies . . . . I figured the heat was
terrible, and she probably had cancer, and—I don't know I
don't care where an actor acts. It can be in summer stock, it
can be in a goddamn Broadway theatre, complete with the
most fashionable, most well-fed, most sunburned-looking au-
dience you can imagine. But I'll tell you a terrible secret . . . .
There isn't anyone out there who isn't Seymour's Fat Lady.

— J.D. SALINGER, *FRANNY AND ZOOEY*

Don't let anyone tell you that what you do is unimportant. Don't
let anyone dismiss you because you are an actor, an artist. It may
not be a cure for cancer, it may not be brain surgery, but we've
dedicated just as many hours of blood, sweat, tears and hard
work to our craft as has any internist. Acting is *our* brain surgery.
And, there in the dark, when what we do is working, it helps an
audience to forget its pain, its sorrow, its grief for a couple of
hours, and reminds all of them of their humanity. What brain sur-
geon can claim that?

Rome was not built in a day.   — JOHN HEYWOOD

Regret for the things we did can be tempered by time; it is re-
gret for the things we did not do that is inconsolable.

— SIDNEY J. HARRIS

Finally, go easy on yourself. Most acting careers don't happen overnight. On average, it takes a minimum of three years to get a career going: finding an agent, getting settled, making connections, meeting casting directors and really getting to know the city. Don't beat yourself up if it doesn't happen in the first six weeks. Or the first year, or two years. Countless actors I know gave up after only a few months. Don't give your career a deadline. Throw away the I-need-to-make-it-by-the-time-I'm-such-and-such-an-age-or-I'll-have-to-find-something-else-to-do thinking and get out there and persevere. Remind yourself daily why you're an actor—which is, presumably, because you love it (how many people in other professions can say that???); because there is nothing else you can or want to do; because it is your "calling."

Index of
Actor Resources

Acting and Performance Related Unions, Guilds and Organizations

Acting Unions

Actors' Equity Association
165 West 46th Street
New York, NY 10036
212-869-8530
www.actorsequity.org

American Federation of Television and Radio Actors
260 Madison Avenue, 7th Floor
New York, NY 10016
212-532-0800
www.aftra.org

American Guild of Musical Artists
1430 Broadway, 14th Floor
New York, NY 10019
212-265-3687
www.musicalartists.org

American Guild of Variety Artists
363 Seventh Avenue, 17th Floor
New York, NY 10001
212-675-1003

Screen Actors Guild
360 Madison Avenue, 12th Floor
New York, NY 10017
212-944-1030
www.sag.org

Acting and Performance-Related Unions, Guilds and Organizations

The Actors' Fund of America
729 Seventh Avenue, 10th Floor
New York, NY 10019
212-221-7300
www.actorsfund.org

The Actors' Work Program
729 Broadway, 11th Floor
New York, NY 10036
212-354-5480

American Federation of Musicians
1501 Broadway, Suite 600
New York, NY 10036
212-869-1330
www.afm.org

Associated Actors and Artistes of America
165 West 46th Street, Room 500
New York, NY 10036
212-869-0358

Association of Theatrical Press Agents and Managers
1560 Broadway, Suite 700
New York, NY 10036
212-719-3666
www.atpam.com

Broadway Cares/Equity Fights AIDS
165 West 46th Street, Suite 1300
New York, NY 10036
212-840-0770
www.bcefa.org

Career Transition for Dancers (CTFD)
The Caroline and Theodore Newhouse Center for Dancers
165 West 46th Street, Suite 701
New York, NY 10036
212-764-0172
www.careertransition.org

Directors Guild of America
110 West 57th Street
New York, NY 10019
212-581-0370
www.dga.org

Dramatists Guild of America
1501 Broadway, Suite 701
New York, NY 10036
212-398-9366
www.dramaguild.com

Episcopalian Actors' Guild of America
1 East 29th Street
New York, NY 10016
212-685-2927
www.actorsguild.org

Guild of Italian American Actors (GIAA)
31 East 32nd Street, 12th Floor
New York, NY 10016-5509
212-420-6590
www.nygiaa.org

Hebrew Actors Union
31 East 7th Street
New York, NY 10003
212-674-1923

Hispanic Organization of Latin Actors (HOLA)
107 Suffolk Street, Suite 302
New York, NY 10002
212-253-1015
www.hellohola.org

**International Alliance of Theatrical Stage Employees
    (IATSE)**
1430 Broadway, 20th Floor
New York, NY 10018
212-730-1770
www.iatse-intl.org

International Photographers of Motion Pictures Industries
80 Eighth Avenue, 14th Floor
New York, NY 10011
212-647-7300

League of Independent Stuntplayers
P.O. Box 196
Madison Square Station
New York, NY 10159
212-777-7021

League of Professional Theatre Women
35 West 64th Street, #4D
New York, NY 10023
646-505-1822
www.theatrewomen.org

**National Association of Broadcast Employees and Technicians
    (NABET)**
80 West End Avenue, 5th Floor
New York, NY 10023
212-757-7191

Police Actors Association
208 West 30th Street, Room 202
New York, NY 10001
212-631-9933

Society of Stage Directors and Choreographers (SSDC)
1501 Broadway, #1701
New York, NY 10036
212-391-1070
www.ssdc.org

United Scenic Artists
29 West 38th Street, 15th Floor
New York, NY 10018
212-581-0300
www.usa829.org

Writers Guild of America (WGA)
555 West 57th Street, Suite 1230
New York, NY 10019
212-767-7800
www.wgaeast.org

Answering Services and Pagers

Aardvark Answering Service
545 Eight Avenue, Room 401
New York, NY 10018
212-626-9000

Actorfone
545 Eighth Avenue, Room 401
New York, NY 10018
212-502-0666

Bells Are Ringing
545 Eighth Avenue, Room 401
New York, NY 10018
212-714-3888

City Never Sleeps
545 Eighth Avenue, Room 401
New York, NY 10018
212-714-5500

Procommunications
445 West 45th Street
New York, NY 10036
212-245-4900

Bookstores

Applause Theater and Cinema Books (211 West 71st Street, just off Broadway—212-496-7511), the little drama bookshop that could, carries a small but good selection of scripts, screenplays and film and theater related books, periodicals and magazines. Unlike the city's other theatrical bookstores, Applause has an inventory of discounted used volumes, occasional reductions on select titles and periodic sales (when I was there last, all hardcovers were 20 percent off).

The Drama Book Shop (250 West 40th Street, between Seventh and Eighth Avenues—212-944-0595) is the best theatrical bookstore in the city, perhaps the country. If it is in print and has anything to do with the theater, you can find it here. Besides carrying just about any play ever published, The Drama Book Shop has a huge selection of books devoted to theater-related subjects, ranging from stage makeup and design to dialects, history and drama therapy. You'll find a very good assortment of books on film and video, as well as lots of industry newspapers and magazines, agent and casting director mailing labels, and DVDs of acclaimed theatrical performances. The very helpful and friendly staff (I assume most are actors) is put through rigorous training. This store, which I consider "actor church," is a sanctuary for anyone who works in, or is passionate about, the theater.

Samuel French (45 West 25th Street—212-206-8990), the world's foremost publisher of plays for over 170 years, has a modest-sized drama bookshop in the foyer of its offices in Chelsea. The books range from film to theater, with lots of acting editions, even those published by its competitors. Pick up a free copy of Samuel French's catalog, which lists all the plays and musicals it publishes.

For those out of the loop, **Theatre Circle** (268 West 44th Street, near Eighth Avenue—212-391-7075) looks like another of the many tourist-oriented shops scattered throughout the Theater District. It does carry an abundance of *Ragtime* refrigerator magnets, *Kiss Me Kate* key rings, *Mamma Mia* coffee mugs and "I ♥ NY" mouse pads, in an attempt to warm the hearts of visitors from Bummerville, CA, Tarzan, TX, Ben Hur, VA, Truth or Consequences, NM, Frankenstein, MO, and Monkeys Eyebrow, KY. Pass the tchotchkes quickly, head to the back room and you will find an outstanding assortment of scripts and theater books. I love this place because they always have what I'm looking for. Frequently, after my agents call with an audition, by the time I arrive at The Drama Book Shop or Applause to pick up a copy of the play, it is sold out. Not so at Theatre Circle; since so few actors know about the back room, this store rarely runs out of stock. Prices here on acting editions are exactly what you'd pay at the other drama book vendors.

Conrad Cantzen Shoe Fund

Shoes are probably the most important item of clothing in our closets, especially since we traverse the city mostly on our feet. Our shoes need to be sturdy, well crafted, provide support and, New York being Fashion Central, have at least a little style. Therefore, shoe expense should be the one corner we are not willing to cut—not that it's easy to find good, cheap shoes.

Fortunately, actors can augment the cost of shoes by taking advantage of the **Conrad Cantzen Memorial Shoe Fund** for performing artists. In 1945, actor Conrad Cantzen died and provided in his will that part of his estate be put into a fund toward allowing performers to buy a new pair of shoes annually. Cantzen believed that performers were more confident when auditioning in new shoes and that a good pair was necessary in an actor's daily round of auditions. Overseen by the Actors' Fund of America, the Cantzen Shoe Fund lets actors purchase a new pair of shoes from a shoe store for up to but not exceed $80. The applicant is then reimbursed up to, but not over $40. To apply to the Shoe Fund, the following requirements must be met:

- You are currently unemployed in the performing profession.

- You are a current, paid-up member of a performing arts union.

- It has been at least a year since you last applied.

If you can meet all the criteria, call or write the Actors' Fund (729 Seventh Avenue, 10th Floor, New York, NY 10019—212-221-7300, www.actorsfund.org) and request an application for the Conrad Cantzen Memorial Shoe Fund. Once you receive the application, fill it out, attach a copy of your current union card and the original printed store receipt for your shoes and send it back. After the application is approved, a check will be mailed to you in approximately 90 days. Note: The Shoe Fund cannot accept written credit-card receipts that do not have a breakdown of your purchase. Also, your shoes must be purchased within the year in which you are applying.

Computer Training

As actors, we don't need to know how to operate a computer, right? Not so many years ago, I agreed with that sentiment, was computer illiterate and proud of it. Claiming that my brain was just too full to make room for the computer stuff I'd have to retain, I resisted getting a computer.

What a difference a few years makes. Today, I would not know how to survive without it. My entire life is on my computer—everything from my personal finances to resumes, teaching materials to address books, stationery, press, personal and business correspondence to pictures, even this book, all live on my hard drive.

I think that owning a computer (and knowing how to use it) is almost as important as owning a phone. Not only does it allow actors to communicate with the world via e-mail, but it can also be our most valuable marketing tool. With a computer, we can create our acting resume, stationery, press releases, mass mailings and mail merges, agent queries, business cards and address books. We can download plays via the internet, research playwrights, actors, directors, theaters, and even receive audition sides on it.

Moreover, computer skills are in demand and companies throw lots of money at those who can do data entry or web design, use Excel spreadsheets or PowerPoint presentations and create Word documents. Between acting jobs, sitting at a computer terminal does a lot less wear-and-tear on the soul and body (and often pays more) than waiting tables. Fortunately, there are two resources that train performing artists, at no charge, how to operate these terrifying but wonderful machines:

The Actors' Work Program (729 Seventh Avenue, between 48th and 49th Streets, 11th Floor—212-354-5480, www.actorsfund.org/human/work.html) schedules several no-cost computer skills courses. To enroll, you need to be a member of one of the entertainment industry unions in good standing and to have attended a Monday afternoon orientation meeting. Program courses include:

- **Basic Computer Fundamentals:** gives AWP members with little or no computer experience fundamental knowledge, such as computer terminology, creating and saving a file and printing a document.

- **Keyboard Skills Class:** improves members' keyboard skills and speed. The class meets for nine hours a week for three weeks.

- **Microsoft Word:** a five-week, three-sessions-per-week intensive class, that develops members' skills using word software and general office work. Prerequisite: typing speed of 50 words per minute and a basic computer skills test.

- **Microsoft Excel and PowerPoint:** a three-week, three-sessions-per-week class, in which members learn how to create and manipulate spreadsheets, and develop a PowerPoint presentation. Prerequisite: typing speed of fifty words per minute and a basic computer skills test.

Call The Actors' Work Program and speak to a career counselor about enrolling in these free classes.

With its mission to "enrich and secure the lives of workers and their families through education, training and job opportunities," and in coordination with the New York state government, the **Consortium for Worker Education** (www.cwe.org) maintains Worker Career Centers that offer free computer access to practice Microsoft Word, Excel, PowerPoint, Access, typing skills and computer-based training programs. A computer lab facilitator is present at all times to answer any questions you may have. No prior reservations are necessary and, although the lab is on a first-come/first-served basis, there is generally no problem getting a computer. The Consortium conducts half-hour mini-computer workshops on a variety of subjects—everything from how to set margins to how to buy a computer. To utilize this facility, you must be a member of one of the entertainment industry unions, The Actors' Fund or The Actors' Work Program (see section on "Meaningful Interim Work and Career Transition"). There are three CWE labs:

215 West 125th Street, 6th Floor—917-493-7000
168-46 91st Avenue, Jamaica, Queens—718-557-6755
9 Bond Street, 5th Floor, Brooklyn—718-246-5219

🍎 🍎 🍎

Demo Reel Editors

I recommend the following demo reel editors for their competitive pricing and top-of-the-line equipment and services, which include some if not all of the following: all format editing and duplicating, titles, effects, image enhancement and correction, audio mixing, graphics and dubbing. Call for rates and a menu of services:

Full Moon Camera and Editing
20 West 20th Street, Suite 240
New York, NY 10001
917-523-3432
www.fullmoonnyc.com

Image Video NY
356 Seventh Avenue, 2nd Floor
New York, NY 10001
212-594-8599
imagevideo@aol.com

Matthew Reilly
12 Brittany Road
South Hadley, MA 01075
413-627-1002

Solar Film and Video
632 Broadway
New York, NY 10012
212-473-3040

Tribeca Lab
401 Broadway
New York, NY 10013
917-587-5392

Videolife Productions
27 West 20th Street
New York, NY 10011

Video Portfolios Productions, Inc.
12 West 27th Street
New York, NY 10001
212-725-3505

Directories

The two preferred performer directories in which you may list yourself for a fee are:

Academy Player's Directory
133 North Vine Street
Los Angeles, CA 90028
310-247-3058
www.playersdirectory.com

Players' Guide
123 West 44th Street, Suite 2J
New York, NY 10036
212-302-9474
www.playersguideny.com

For a full description of actor directories, see the chapter on "Mailings and Marketing."

Free and Discounted Theater and Film

Besides bringing us a lot of joy (hopefully), regularly attending plays and films is beneficial for our craft and our careers. However critical it is for us to go to the movies and see theater, both are expensive. Every season, ticket prices go up, shutting out modestly paid actors from attending. Luckily, there are a few "for actors only" ways to beat the high price of film and theater-going without having to resort to seeing only deconstructed Wedekind plays performed in taxidermists' lofts on the Lower East Side or your best friend's PowerPoint presentation of his trip to Rochester:

Actors' Equity occasionally is given complimentary Broadway, off-Broadway and showcase tickets to distribute to its members. There is no rhyme or reason as to when these freebies are disbursed. Since it is at the producer's discretion and needs that they are given to Equity, weeks can go by with no comps at all. Whenever you are in midtown, it won't hurt to run up to the second floor members' lounge to check on availability. Actors' Equity Association, 165 West 46th Street at Seventh Avenue, 2nd floor Members' Lounge.

Use your Equity card to gain entrance into any **AEA Approved Showcase** in the city. These plays, usually produced on a minuscule budget and in some of New York's funkier theater spaces, are meant to showcase the talents of theater artists to the people who will be hiring them or finding them work. Because struggling individuals or companies with next-to-no money produce these, Equity allows actors to work for no pay. In return, AEA members may view these shows at no cost. You can find a list of these off-off-Broadway shows in the "Cue" section of *New York Magazine*, in *Time Out New York*, or the "Sunday Arts and Leisure" section of *The New York Times*. (For more information, check out the "Showcases" chapter.)

The best way to see theater is to network with your friends and colleagues. You're an actor, right? You know actors and theater professionals, right? You probably know actors and theater professionals who are doing shows right now, right? Tell any actor, director, designer, producer, usher, house-manager, dresser, stage-manager, crew person and ticket booth employee you know who is doing a show that if the theater is **"papering,"** to count you in. "Papering" a house is a practice most producers use in which free tickets are disbursed so that the actors and creative team can determine how the show plays in front of a full audience. At the same time, producers don't want audience members who paid full price to see a lot of empty seats and worry that they have spent their money on a turkey.

Paid-up members of **Screen Actors Guild** in good standing have three ways they can get into a movie for little or no money. The "no money" way first:

1. The Screen Actors Guild Awards, which are considered one of the

industry's most prized honors, presents thirteen awards for acting in film and television. The awards acknowledge the greatness of both individual performers as well as the work of the ensemble of a drama and comedy series and the cast of a motion picture. The SAG Awards are unique in the composition of its voters. Two randomly selected panels of 2100 SAG members choose the nominees for television and motion pictures. The final ballot of nominees is then sent out to the entire active SAG membership (over 98,000 members), who votes their choice for the outstanding performances of the year. From November through January of each year, those SAG members who are fortunate enough to be chosen for the SAG nominating committee, together with a guest, may view for free just about any movie at just about any theater. All you need to do is show your SAG Nominating Committee card and a picture ID at the Box Office. Keep your fingers crossed that you are lucky enough to be chosen for the nominating committee. Even if you don't have that privilege (I haven't yet—ugh!), there is still a window of about six weeks after the nominations are announced when you and a guest can see any of the nominated films for free. To view the nominated films, show your valid SAG card and a picture ID at the Box Office. For a list of award-nominated films, check the ballot that is sent to you in February or the SAG website (www.sag.com). During February and early March, check any New York newspapers' ads to see if SAG members are given free entry.

2. About twice a year, the three major film chains—AMC, UA and Sony/Loews/Magic Johnson—each offer a limited number of discount coupons to all Screen Actors Guild members. These coupons, which are $5 each, may only be purchased at the SAG offices (360 Madison Avenue, 12th Floor) from 9:30 A.M. to 4:30 P.M. They are valid for a year from the date of purchase, may be used at any participating theater nationwide and are good for any show time except during "special engagements," generally within the first ten days of a new release. Pay for coupons by cash, money order or cashiers check only. Although there is no official distribution date for the coupons, they are usually released in April and September. This offer is on a first-come/first-served basis—SAG is allotted a finite number of tickets; once those are sold out, there are no more until the follow-

ing distribution period. The Guild's monthly newsletter informs members of the coupon sale; you may also call the Business Office (212-944-1030) and ask the date of the next distribution. You are allowed to purchase a maximum of fifty coupons per person per day; you must show your paid-up SAG card at the time of purchase. (Note: AMC and Sony/Loews/Magic Johnson cinemas charge a $1 surcharge. Even with the surcharge, $6 (which is approximately what the rest of the country is paying) is a hell of a lot better than $10 to see a movie.)

3. For $95, the Screen Actors Guild Film Society of New York offers its members and a guest the opportunity to see twenty "first-run" films. The Film Society, which functions as a showcase for "contemporary products of the film industry," presents these films through the courtesy of the distributors at no cost to the Society. Your nominal membership is used to defray operating costs. To become a member of the Society, either walk in and pick up or call and request an application from the SAG Committee Office (360 Madison Avenue, 12th Floor— 212-944-1030). You must correctly fill out and sign the application and return it with your signed check. Your Film Society membership card will be sent the last week in August; the screenings begin in September. All Film Society screenings are held at the Directors Guild of America (110 West 57th Street, between Sixth and Seventh Avenues) on Mondays and Tuesdays at 1 P.M., 3:30 P.M., 6 P.M., and 8:30 P.M. You may request the day and time you would like, but if you want an evening screening act fast as they fill up quickly.

Committed to building audiences and supporting the performing arts in New York City, the **Theatre Development Fund (TDF)** oversees several different discount ticket programs. Of particular interest to actors are TDF's discounts offered to members via snail- and e-mail. The savings under this program are tremendous—as much as 75 percent or more for both Broadway and off-Broadway shows. To be eligible for membership, you must be one of the following: student, teacher, union member, retired person, performing arts professional, clergy, or member of the armed forces. Along with its great services, TDF sends quarterly newsletters and periodic e-mail updates of available shows, also maintains a website where you can find everything you need to know about its programs, and provides information by phone on all theater, dance and music events in the city (212-768-1818). Eligible applicants may write to TDF (enclosing a self-addressed stamped envelope) for an application form at 1501 Broadway, New York, NY 10036 (212-221-0013). You may also download and fill out the form online (www.tdf.org). Either way, you must provide proof of eligibility and pay an annual processing fee of $22.50 (only $15 for members of the acting unions during their first year on the mailing list).

At the **Vineyard Theatre** (108 East 15th Street—212-353-0303, www.vineyardtheatre.org), professional performing artists who show a paid-up union card may, at the beginning of the theatre's season (usually early fall), purchase a membership for only $15 and then pay just $10 per show for the entire season. Call for more details.

Getting Help and Health Services

Given the unpredictability of our employment, our lives and our health, we may find we need assistance with financial difficulties as well as housing, legal matters, childcare, health and insurance concerns, chemical dependency, senior and disabled care, and career transition. Fortunately, there are organizations and programs established to provide free/discounted, compassionate, confidential assistance to all professionals in the entertainment community.

Actors' Equity Association (165 West 46th Street at Broadway— 212-869-8530, www.actorsequity.org) assists members with up to $300 for general living expenses such as rent, food, utilities and medical expenses. To be eligible, you must be a member in good standing and have at least three years of Equity earnings.

A few years ago I had hurt my back and was laid up for several weeks. I saw a series of specialists, surgeons and physical therapists and received conflicting diagnoses. I had to have X-rays and a very expensive MRI; my treatment called for three pricey nerve root blocks. With each consultation and treatment, my medical debt soared to unmanageable levels.

Ultimately, my back problems were healed so that I could walk and work again, but I was left with crippling debt, even after my insurance paid the portion of the bills they deemed "reasonable and customary." I was scared and did not know where to turn. Then, a friend told me about the program overseen by **The Actors' Fund of America** that was established to help members of the entertainment industry who find themselves in crisis. The benevolence from this organization helped me reduce my otherwise bankrupting medical debt; they also referred me to AFTRA, which assisted with my bills as well.

PRICELESS RESOURCE

Founded in 1882, The Actors' Fund (729 Seventh Avenue at 49th Street, 10th Floor—212-221-7300, www.actorsfund.org) is the only national, nonprofit human service organization that provides for the welfare of all entertainment professionals—designers, writers, sound technicians, musicians, dancers, administrators, directors, film editors, stagehands, as well as actors. Professionals in film, television, radio, theater, dance and music all are eligible for The Actors' Fund services in times of need. To apply for assistance or to utilize the services of The Actors' Fund, you must document earnings made as a performer or in a performing related field. The many confidential programs The Actors' Fund oversees to address the needs of the acting community include social services, vocational counseling, financial assistance, supportive housing and medical care.

The Actors' Fund social services, developed and administered by a staff of social workers, include:

- **Entertainment Industry Assistance Program**—offering counseling on a broad range of issues from career transitions to the challenges of aging in the entertainment industry and family and work matters. This program provides advocacy and referrals on housing, legal, childcare, and health services needs; assists financially on an emergency basis for living and health expenses; schedules workshops throughout the year on such topics as budgeting, securing affordable housing, debt management, investments, taxes and estate planning.

- **Chemical Dependency Program**—helping individuals and families address substance abuse and addiction with the goal of achieving and maintaining sobriety.

- **Mental Health Services**—offering psychological evaluation, crisis intervention and counseling, as well as referrals to clinics, hospitals, and sliding scale or reduced rate psychotherapists who are familiar with the needs of the entertainment industry.

- **Phyllis Newman Women's Health Initiative**—providing counseling, support services and financial assistance toward healthcare and insurance costs for women who are coping with significant health problems.

- **AIDS Initiative**, with the generous support of **Broadway Cares/Equity Fights AIDS**—providing care management, counseling, support groups, referral, emergency and ongoing financial assistance for medical treatment, housing and other basic needs for persons with HIV/AIDS and their loved ones.

- **Senior Care Program**—helps industry members in their "golden" years by providing information on community resources for medical/dental care, housing, assisted living and skilled care. The Actors' Fund social workers also provide elder-care counseling and support services for families and make home and hospital visits to coordinate health maintenance.

- **Disabled Care Program**—providing support for those who are living with short- and long-term illness or disability.

The **Actors' Fund Health Services** include:

- **Artists' Health Insurance Resource Center (AHIRC)**—Because many performers do not receive health insurance through employment and do not qualify for needs-based insurance, they frequently fall through the cracks. In response to this crisis, the National Endowment for the Arts, in partnership with The Actors' Fund of America, have established the **Artists' Health Insurance Resource Center**. The AHIRC assists the arts community nationwide in accessing information about health insurance options. Go to The Actors' Fund website at **www.actorsfund.org/ahirc**, where you'll find information about several government-subsidized programs and consumer organizations that offer quality affordable healthcare coverage options. The information available includes: guides to purchasing insurance; artists' groups offering health insurance; a list of free and sliding scale clinics; healthcare options for the uninsured and underinsured; sources of emergency financial aid for medical/hospital bills; plans for the self-employed; access to group health insurance; and guides to gaining disease-specific assistance. Individuals may also receive health insurance advice and counseling through The Actors' Fund offices or through the AHIRC toll free helpline—800-798-8447.

- Established in 2003 by The Actors' Fund of America, **The Al Hirschfeld Free Health Clinic** (The Aurora, 475 West 57th Street, 2nd Floor—212-489-1939, www.actorsfund.org) is a free medical clinic providing quality health care for all uninsured and underinsured entertainment professionals in the New York City area. For continuity care, a full-time family physician is on-site at the clinic four days a week. The clinic also has a group of practitioners and specialists who volunteer their time to provide a variety of medical services. In cases where a specialty consultation is necessary, The Al Hirschfeld Free Health Clinic makes low cost referrals to a wide range of clinics and practitioners throughout the region. Additional Al Hirschfeld Free Clinic services include: ongoing information on wellness issues; laboratory testing; blood pressure and cholesterol screenings; gynecological examinations; prostate examinations; annual health fairs; vision screening; flu shots; women's health fair; mammograms; colon/rectal cancer screening; PSA blood levels; electrocardiograms; and an on-call physician when the clinic is closed. All documented entertainment professionals with a union card from within one year or other documentation (call for details), who have no health insurance or cannot afford their deductible or an indemnity plan are eligible for clinic services. Those actors currently employed but in need of urgent care may also utilize the clinic. To make an appointment, call Monday to Friday between 9:30 A.M. and 5 P.M.

The Actors' Fund Employment and Training Services include:

- **AIDS Training and Education Project**—assisting AIDS Initiative clients who wish to explore transitioning to work, school and volunteering.

- **Act II**—addressing the specific career training needs of entertainment professionals over fifty.

The Actors' Fund Supportive Housing programs include:

- **Affordable Housing Residences**—oversees The Aurora building (see chapter on "Finding a Home").

- **Actors' Fund Homes**—providing assisted living and skilled nursing care for retired entertainment professionals and their immediate family members in a comfortable environment.

American Guild of Musical Artists (AGMA) Relief Fund (1727 Broadway at 55th Street—212-265-3687, www.musicalartists.org) provides monetary assistance to members who are needy, aged, infirm or unable to meet financial obligations. The Relief Fund also assists members in need of counseling, medical or legal referrals.

American Guild of Variety Artists (AGVA) Fund (363 Seventh Avenue at 30th Street, 17th Floor—212-675-1003) offers financial aid to members who are ill, elderly or indigent to pay for rent, utilities and medical bills.

The **Episcopalian Actors' Guild of America, Inc.** (1 East 29th Street between Fifth and Madison Avenues—212-685-2927, www.actorsguild.org) offers emergency financial aid to performing arts professionals to help cover rent, utilities, union dues, moving and storage fees and medical expenses. You don't need to be an Episcopalian to apply, but you must be a working member of the theatrical profession (union membership is not necessary) and first go through the application process at your parent union and/or other agencies like The Actors' Fund to be eligible for grants from the Guild. Call the Guild for full eligibility requirements.

For almost twenty years **The Miller Health Care Institute for the Performing Arts at St. Luke's/Roosevelt Hospital** (425 West 59th Street, between Ninth and Tenth Avenues, Suite 6—212-523-6200, www.millerinstitute.org) has been providing affordable general and specialized medical care for performing artists, as well as those in allied professions such as teachers, coaches, designers, writers, directors and production crews. Designed for and dedicated to the specific health needs of performing artists, The Miller Institute is also sensitive to each performer's budgetary constrictions—uninsured and underinsured patients are offered quality care on a sliding scale. The Institute also accepts Medicare and has several grants to expand access to their specialty programs (for more information about grants, contact The Miller Institute or consult their website). Institute services encompass everything from routine checkups and diagnosis and treatment of acute and chronic medical problems to specialized care like acupuncture, psychotherapy, dance medicine, speech therapy, physical rehabilitation, orthopedics, massage therapy and nutrition. Unique to the Institute are its voice laboratory to examine ailing vocal chords; a physical therapy gym with a sprung dance floor, ballet barres and mirrors; and a performance evaluation studio to examine musicians' performance problems and progress. Patients are seen by appointment only, but some slots are open every day for those with urgent medical problems.

Screen Actors Guild Foundation (360 Madison Avenue at East 45th Street—212-944-1030, www.sag.org) provides emergency assistance to cover rent/mortgage, utilities and car insurance/car payments for paid-up members who are sick, needy, indigent or aged. The SAG Foundation also assists members with medical expenses if they have no medical coverage.

The **Theatre Authority Fund at AFTRA** (260 Madison Avenue, between East 38th and 39th Streets, 7th Floor—212-532-0800, www.aftra.org) assists any paid-up AFTRA member who is in need of financial help. Theatre Authority Fund grants are for living expenses only (rent, utilities, food, travel, medical, etc.). Members applying for assistance must show just cause why they are in need of financial help. Maximum assistance per year is $1,000, but there is no limit on how many times a member may apply.

The **Unemployment and Workers' Compensation Office at Actors' Equity Association** (165 West 46th Street—212-869-8530, ext. 327, www.actorsequity.org) is a little-known division of AEA, which can be a real lifesaver for members who have trouble collecting unemployment or been hurt while working. The office counsels and advises members on initial unemployment insurance filings and trouble-shoots on pending claims.

Twice this office has intervened on my behalf when the New York State Department of Labor delayed my claim; each time, their call resulted in the immediate disbursal of my benefits. The Unemployment and Workers' Compensation Office has a comprehensive understanding of the differing unemployment laws in all fifty states (since we work all over the country) and can answer questions regarding Combined Wage Claims, Interstate Claims, Interstate Combined Wage Claims, and eligibility requirements.

In connection with workers' compensation claims, the office advises and assists members in obtaining information on coverage. They trouble-shoot if an injured member's lost time benefits are held up, and keep an updated file on compensation coverage for individual theaters and shows. Also, in tandem with the Equity League Health Trust Fund, the office provides a Supplemental Workers' Compensation Plan for performers who are injured on the job and who lose time and salary as a result. To qualify for this benefit, you must be eligible and apply for workers' compensation. If you qualify for workers' compensation, the Fund gives additional compensation. Call for more information.

Headshot Reproduction Services

For dependability, quality of work and competitive pricing, I consider the following the superior headshot reproduction labs in the metropolitan area:

Alluring Images
208 West 29th Street, Suite 408
New York, NY 10001
212-967-1610
www.alluringimages.com

AV Studios
36 West 20th Street, 6th Floor
New York, NY 10011
917-715-3231

Guttenberg Printing
237 West 54th Street, 4th Floor
New York, NY 10019
212-333-3033

Ideal Photos of NYC
155 West 46th Street, 11th Floor
New York, NY 10036
212-575-0303

JB Photo Services
307 West 37th Street
New York, NY 10018
212-244-6959

Modern Age Photo Labs
1150 Avenue of the Americas
New York, NY 10030
212-997-1800
www.modernage.com/headshots.html

N.E. Photo & Design
224 West 30th Street, 11th Floor
New York, NY 10001
212-563-1646
www.nephotoanddesign.com

Precision Photos
750 Eighth Avenue
New York, NY 10036
212-302-2724; 800-583-4077
www.precisionphotos.com

Reproductions
6 West 37th Street, 4th Floor
New York, NY 10018
212-967-2568; 800-647-3776
www.reproductions.com/NYC

Ken Taranto Studios
38 East 30th Street, 2nd Floor
New York, NY 10016
(212) 691-6070; 800-556-3914
www.tarantolabs.com

Investing Information

Gary Ginsberg of **Royal Alliance Associates, Inc. NASD, SIPC** has an office at the Actors Federal Credit Union (165 West 46th Street, 4th Floor—212-869-8926, ext. 315, www.actorsfcu.org), and helps actors understand the importance of beginning an investment program and the intricacies involved. As Gary says, "We applaud and respect actors for their capacity to be creative. They are trained to nurture right-brained thinking—to be free of the bounds of conventional thought. Yet, one of the most undeniable practical concerns of modern life is the left-brained necessity of 'personal finance,' and actors generally are not taught how to manage money. The ultimate irony of leading a creative life is that actors MUST address the financial aspect of their lives. They run their own business and typically will not have a 401 (k), corporate savings plan, substantive pension, or even health or life insurance, which is often provided by an employer. If an actor does not take care of his or her own finances, no one is going to do it for them."

Through his services, Gary helps performing artists evaluate their personal financial situation, and then educates them on what investment options correlate directly to their financial goals and risk tolerance. Gary believes that the only way to achieve these goals is by understanding that investing for the future is not a one-time event, but rather a lifelong process, which should be reviewed on an ongoing basis when goals, risks, taxes, financial circumstances, or investment allocations change.

For a lot of actors, taking the first step is the hardest. Gary constantly hears, "I can't afford it right now. I don't have enough at the end of the month to invest." Gary replies, "Change your attitude! If you don't start at the level you are at today, you will never start." His philosophy is: Instead of looking at monthly investments as a luxury, **pay yourself first.** The first check you write each month should be to yourself; when you get into this habit you will become an investor for life. He adds, "Act once a month as if you're left-brained and financial freedom is a goal you can reach!" Gary holds his office at AFCU on Tuesdays and Thursdays. You must call for an appointment.

Lawyers

A time may come when you will need a lawyer, but won't be able to afford exorbitant legal fees. A few alternatives offer legal assistance either at no cost or at greatly reduced rates:

Established for the exclusive use of members of participating AFL-CIO unions and their families, **Union Plus Legal Services** provides free or low-cost legal assistance to members of Equity. Call or go by the Equity offices (165 West 46th Street, 15th Floor—212-869-8530, www.unionpriv.org/benefits/legal) and ask for a list of participating Union Plus lawyers in the New York metropolitan area. Benefits through Union Plus include:

- **Free thirty-minute consultation** by phone or at the attorney's office on any personal legal matter you choose. There is no limit on the number of consultations, provided each is about a separate matter.

- **Free review of important documents** such as leases, insurance policies, etc., followed by an oral explanation of the terms of these documents. (Note: Written evaluations are *not* part of this service, nor are documents written by you or for use in a business capacity.)

- **Free follow-up services** by phone or letter to help you resolve a problem or dispute you may have.

- **Confidentiality**—only your attorney knows you are using the program.

- **Thirty percent discount** on more complex legal matters. In a contingent fee case (where the lawyer's fee comes out of any recovery or award you obtain), or on a business matter, a smaller discount may apply. Otherwise, flat fees usually apply to commonly needed services.

- **Written agreement on all fees** to prevent any financial surprises.

All lawyers participating in the Union Plus program are selected for their involvement in the labor movement and their interest in serving union members. They have agreed to provide all program benefits (both free and discounted), to keep each member fully informed of the status of his or her case, and to abide by the administrative responsibilities required of them.

To insure your satisfaction with the program and the quality of its participating attorneys, Union Plus asks you to evaluate the services of your lawyer. Should you disagree with your lawyer regarding fees or other matters, Union Plus tries to resolve the dispute through informal mediation, or, if necessary, arbitration. (Note: Because this is a union program, matters involving any union-related organization or official are not included. Furthermore, a Union Plus attorney may refuse to take any case as he or she so chooses.)

Each year, **Volunteer Lawyers for the Arts (VLA)** (1 East 53rd Street, 6th Floor—212-319-2787, www.vlany.org) provides pro bono and low-cost legal services to over 5,000 members of the creative community in the greater New York metropolitan area. Since 1969, the group has assisted artists with mediation services, educational programs and publications, advocacy, legal advice, professional business counseling, and representation. Included in VLA's many services are:

- **Art Law Line**—a free legal hotline.

- **Pro bono placements** for low-income artists and nonprofit arts organizations with volunteer attorneys from the area's finest law firms

• **Low-cost membership** ($50 for full-time students, $100 for individuals and $200 for nonprofit arts organizations) entitling members to half-hour appointments with highly qualified volunteer attorneys to address arts-related legal issues at the group's bi-monthly clinics. Membership also covers discounts on seminars, workshops, publications and MediateArt Services; invitations to all Member Events; VLA Newsletter; access to the Speaker's Bureau and VLA's Board Bank; and discounts on pro bono consultations for those who meet VLA's Financial Eligibility Guidelines.

• **Workshops** on specific legal topics related to the arts, such as:
  • Nonprofit Incorporation and Tax Exempt Status
  • Artists Rights and New Technology
  • Starting and Operating a For-Profit Business
  • Starting and Operating an Independent Record Label
  • Contract Basics For Arts and Entertainment Professionals
  • Copyright Basics
  • Mediation Training

• **Assistance with Nonprofit Incorporation**

Telephone for more information on VLA's services and membership, or for a schedule of workshops.

If you have questions or need help with problems of discrimination in the workplace or housing due to sexual orientation or HIV/AIDS, contact the **Lambda Legal Help Line** (212-809-8585, www.lambdalegal.org) for free guidance on rights and recourse. Lambda's Help Line is open on weekdays from 9 A.M. to 5:30 P.M.

The **Metropolitan Council on Housing Help Line** (212-979-0611, www.metrocouncil.org/housing/housing) is set up to answer any questions you may have regarding apartments, leases, landlords, renter's rights, etc. This free service, staffed by legal professionals, can be accessed on Mondays, Wednesdays and Fridays from 1:30 P.M. to 5 P.M.

Mailing Labels

Casting List
c/o Showbiz LTD.
8721 Santa Monica Boulevard
West Hollywood, CA 90069
877-570-9662
www.castinglist.com

Henderson Labels
212-472-2292
www.hendersonenterprises.com

Pro-Labels
212-592-1902
www.prolabels.com

Makeup

Actors, with proof of eligibility (see below for details), are entitled to discounts at the following makeup retailers:

Because it caters to the theatrical industry and professional makeup artists, everything at **Alcone** (235 West 19th Street—212-633-0551 and 5-49 49th Avenue, Long Island City—718-361-8373, www.alconeco.com) is always discounted. Alcone's great appeal is that it carries brands not found in any other stores, such as Visiora, RCMA and Kryolan, and has a website where anything from its stock can be ordered. Alcone sells popular theatrical brands like Ben Nye and Mehron, as well as removers, sponges, powder puffs, and palettes. If it is special effects makeup you want, this is the place to go; Alcone has the definitive selection of latex, blood products, bruise kits and scar-making materials in the city. No proof of professional status is needed.

Not as generous as many of the other makeup stores in the city, **Bob Kelly**

Cosmetics (151 West 46th Street, Room 902—212-819-0030, ext. 17) does offer actors a 10 percent discount off all Bob Kelly Theatrical professional makeup. This is the makeup you probably used when you started out as an actor, and there is still no better theatrical base or crème stick on the market. You must show your union card or picture and resume to be eligible for the discount.

On payment of an annual fee of $35, **MAC Cosmetics** stores offer performers a generous 30 percent discount on all products through their "Preferred Professionals" program. To be eligible, you must present photo identification and any two of the following: composite card, valid union card, headshot, program/press materials with name credit, contract on production company letterhead or crew/cast call list on production company letterhead. There are four MAC locations:
   113 Spring Street, between Greene and Mercer Streets—212-334-4641
   202 West 125th Street at Seventh Avenue—212-665-0676
   139 Fifth Avenue, between 20th and 21st Streets—212-505-3563
   767 Fifth Avenue at 22nd Street—212-677-6611
   www.maccosmetics.com

The **Makeup Center** (150 West 55th Street—212-977-9494) stocks a large assortment of theatrical makeup by Ben Nye, Stein's and Mehron, as well as a full line of special effects products such as bald caps, stage blood, blood capsules, crepe hair, latex and glitter. The Makeup Center features its own line of theatrical and regular makeup. By presenting a membership card from any of the acting unions, actors receive a 15 percent discount on all sales.

Meaningful Interim Work and Career Transition

Meeting with a friend recently whom I had not seen in several months, it wasn't long into our reunion when she asked me the inevitable actor-question, "What are you working on now?" My reply: "Well (ahem), I'm between jobs." Without missing a beat, she said, "No, you are between successes."

I liked the implication of that statement. So much of an actor's career is about looking for work, being unemployed, and trying to keep sane during those periods when we are "at large." Adopting the idea of going from success to success acts as a positive buffer to the inevitable downtime we have in our profession.

With nothing else to do that is at all meaningful, except look for the next acting job, that downtime can be brutal. Our egos take a battering; we question our talent, our place and ourselves in the business. And yet, our rent and bills must be paid and we must eat. So, we engage in survival work we hate, which exhausts us emotionally and physically and bashes our egos that much more. And then, of course, we get that acting job and are back on top of the world . . . this is the never-ending cycle of being an actor.

Well, the cycle need not be so dire; there are outlets for us that provide a community around the process of supporting ourselves when we are "between successes." These outlet organizations firmly believe that theater artists can develop parallel talents so that our survival work can excite us as much and be as creative and meaningful as our chosen craft. At the same time, they help the performing artist who has decided to leave the acting profession make a dignified transition among a group of supportive and creative people. If you have ever wondered, "Who am I when I'm not working? How will I manage my time when I'm not working? Who will I be in the future?" these organizations can definitely help you:

The Actors' Work Program (729 Seventh Avenue, between 48th and 49th Street, 11th Floor—212-354-5480, www.actorsfund.org/human/work.html) is one of the best actor support services organizations in the country. The Actors' Work Program, a program under The Actors' Fund of America, has a free, full-service career counseling, education and training center for all members of the entertainment industry unions. Members are offered an opportunity to develop the skills needed to secure meaningful remunerative work while "between successes," or to explore changing career paths.

The Program operates from the idea that all actors possess many talents and skills that are invaluable to the business world and other professions, and helps acting professionals recognize these skills, obtain new ones and prepare for satisfying and financially rewarding employment. Its many no-cost services include:

- **Individual Career Counseling**—to develop the AWP member's individual career plans

- **Resume and Interview Workshop**—personalized help with resume preparation, interview techniques and job search strategies

- **Career Search Spotlight and Other Seminars**—introduces an array of sideline career options including computers, teaching and entrepreneurial ventures; sponsors "career nights," which present a variety of additional fields of interest; offers seminars on returning to school, time management, careers in training, substitute teaching, small business practices, interviewing skills, salaries and other relevant topics.

- **Willard Swire Computer Lab Tutorials**—where members can practice their computer/typing skills and gain access to the internet for job search and career exploration

- **Classes**—includes computer (keyboard, Word, Excel and Power-Point), English as a Second Language, and Arts-In-Education

- **Tuition Grants**—helps eligible members access tuition assistance for specialized training programs

- **Job Search**—Wednesday afternoon seminars help members who are pursuing sideline work by sharing listings of current job openings

- **Job Bulletin Board**—an ever-changing list of currently available job offerings, mainly for people with skills in computers, proofreading, English as a Second Language, etc.

You must be a member of an entertainment industry union and must attend one of their weekly orientation meetings to take advantage of The Actors' Work Program's many services. Orientations take place every Monday from 12:00 noon to 2:30 P.M. and give an overview of AWP's programs. At this time, any basic questions you may have about the Program will be answered and you will be scheduled for an individual appointment with a Program counselor. To get started, call their number or attend one of the Monday orientations.

In 1985, **Career Transition for Dancers (CTFD)** (The Caroline and Theodore Newhouse Center for Dancers, 165 West 46th Street, Suite 701—212-764-0172, www.careertransition.org) was founded to "empower current and former professional dancers with the knowledge and skills necessary to clearly define their career possibilities after dance, and to provide resources necessary to help make these possibilities a reality." CTFD gives dancers tools to help them decide what they want to do after their dance careers have ended and assists them in making a meaningful transition. CTFD's free services and programs include:

Career Counseling—a variety of one-to-one and career counseling programs for eligible dancers to use at every stage of their transition process

Scholarships—grants to retiring dancers so that they may initiate an academic or retraining process in the pursuit of undergraduate, graduate and professional degrees as well as skill and vocational certificates

"Career Conversations"—a series of seminars and workshops on career planning topics and the transition process

"Career Line"—a nationwide toll-free counseling and referral hotline for dancers outside the New York and Los Angeles metropolitan areas

Resources—an ever-changing and expanding array of reference guides, periodicals and other materials, both on-line and off, for dancers to utilize in their transition process

Career Transition for Dancers' services and programs are available to current and former dancers from all disciplines who can demonstrate they earned their livelihood from performing as dancers. (Note: Income earned as a choreographer or dance instructor is not applicable. Call for full eligibility requirements and further information on membership.)

Performing Arts-Related Museums and Research Institutions

In its heyday in the 1920s and '30s, the Astoria Studios that house the **American Museum of the Moving Image** (35th Avenue at 36th Street, Queens—718-784-0077, www.ammi.org) was Paramount Pictures' main East Coast production facility. During World War II, the studios were utilized by the U.S. Army to make training films for wartime inductees; after the war, and up through the 1970s, the site fell into disuse. In the '80s, the facility was renovated into a fully operational studio and museum. The AMMI, dedicated to educating the public about the art, history and technology of film, television and digital media, conserves the country's largest collection of moving image artifacts, including props, costumes, sets, scripts and equipment. The museum's wonderful permanent exhibit, "Behind the Screen," offers an interactive history of the medium, a perspective on how film and television have changed and influenced American history, and an overview of the process of producing, marketing and exhibiting moving images. Throughout the year, the AMMI presents hundreds of film and video screenings, drawn from a wide array of genres, in its three state-of-the-art theaters. Anyone who wants to act in or make films should run, not walk, to this museum. Admission: adults $10; seniors and college students $7.50; members and children under five free. Call or go to the museum's website for hours and a schedule of screenings.

After the Lincoln Center Library for the Performing Arts, the **Donnell Library** (20 West 53rd Street, between Fifth and Sixth Avenues—212-621-0618, www.nypl.org), a branch of the NYPL, has the next best collection of theater and performance-related materials in the city. The Donnell also has a tremendous choice of videos that may be borrowed for up to one week and that comprises most major film categories, including documentary, animated, foreign-language and television (look for the BBC's *Complete Works of William Shakespeare*). Of special interest is the Media Center at the Donnell, which shelves an extensive library of film and videotapes. You may view any of these at the library for free if you make an appointment twenty-four to forty-eight hours in advance. The Media Center also sponsors film screenings every Wednesday and Thursday in the fall, winter and spring and Wednesdays in the summer. Call the Media Center or consult the NYPL website for a complete schedule.

Following its three-year renovation, the **Lincoln Center Library for the Performing Arts** (Lincoln Center—111 Amsterdam Avenue at 66th Street—212-870-1630, www.nypl.org/research/lpa) finally re-opened in 2002 and performers throughout the city are rejoicing. With outstanding research and circulating collections covering all the performing arts from music to dance, theater and film, this place is for us. The library's nine million holdings include books, recordings, videos, sheet music, correspondence, programs, set and costume renderings, scale models, and photographs. Want to read John Gielgud's autobiography? It's here. Want a copy of Tony Kushner's *Angels in America*? It's here. Want to hear a recording of Rex Harrison playing Benedick? It's here. Want to know what Frank Rich said about *Sweeney Todd*? It's here. Want to view John Barton's *Playing Shakespeare* television series? You can do it here.

To me, the Theatre on Film and Tape division is the best part of the library. It holds taped or acquired recordings of thousands of live performances from Broadway, off-Broadway and regional theaters. These have been archived and are available to view. Space is limited, so you must call in advance to reserve the play you'd like to see; expect to wait about two weeks for an opening. Depending on monitor availability, the Theatre on Film and Tape division often allows walk-ins.

Flanked by huge windows that create a feeling of openness and light, the library's renovated reading rooms have several listening units at which users may review CDs and cassette tapes, 200 public-access computers, a sea of desks with electric outlets to plug in laptops, and hundreds of ergonomically designed Aeron chairs make research a luxury. What's more, the library has a state-of-the-art technology training center that offers classes and resources on research in the performing arts, and an updated material retrieval system that allows for simultaneous access to its four research collections.

The Performing Arts Library hosts frequent and free exhibits on the life and work of distinguished actors, choreographers, directors, composers, designers, playwrights, singers, dancers and musicians. This is the best performing arts reference resource in the city, perhaps the world, so USE IT! Its four collections are:

Dance—212-870-1657
Music—212-870-1650/1625
Rodgers & Hammerstein Archives of Recorded Sound—212-870-1663
Sound Recordings, Videos and DVDs—212-870-1625
Theatre on Film and Tape—212-870-1642

All of the objects housed in the **Museum of the City of New York** (1220 Fifth Avenue at 103rd Street—212-534-1672) relate to the history and traditions of New York City. Of special interest to actors is the ongoing show "Broadway! 125 Years of Musical Theatre," which surveys the Great White Way's history through costumes, set models and designs, posters, programs and photographs. Every day except Monday is "Pay-As-You-Wish."

A great resource for actors, and one of my favorite museums is **The Museum of Television and Radio** (25 West 52nd Street, between Fifth and Sixth Avenues—212-621-6800, www.mtr.org). The museum's collection contains more than 95,000 TV and radio programs made over the past seventy years. A computerized catalog system with an enormous database allows the public to review the museum's collection of programs ranging from news to commercials to comedies to dramas and variety shows. I have found it especially helpful as a research tool when I am preparing an audition or role: using its vast database I have viewed everything from TV documentaries about Nazi Germany to portions of "Your Show of Shows" and BBC productions of Shakespeare plays. Throughout the year the museum hosts several film series that focus on topics of social, historical, popular or artistic interest. Ask for a schedule at the front counter. (Note: You are limited to four hours of viewing/listening time per day.)

Famous the world over for the stone lions posted in front of its gorgeous beaux-arts façade, the **New York Public Library—Humanities and Social Sciences Library** (455 Fifth Avenue at 42nd Street—212-869-8089, www.nypl.org) is the main branch of the library system and one of the city's architectural gems. This library, and its outpost branch across the street, has an outstanding collection of scripts, scores and theater-related books. If you're interested in scanning past news articles or reviews, the library has an outstanding newspaper microfilm retrieval system. While there, be sure to check out the Rose Reading Room—about as ostentatious and awe-inspiring a main reading room as anything I've ever seen. If you find yourself at the library on a warm sunny day, sit on the steps out front for some of the best people-watching in New York.

Rose Museum at Carnegie Hall (Seventh Avenue and 57th Street—212-903-9600). This museum houses some of the world-famous concert hall's most cherished memorabilia in its collections and archives, including photographs, letters, autographs, programs, and other items, all chronicling the hall's rich history. Always free.

Performing Arts Union Members Only Discount Programs

There are three outstanding programs in which deep discounts are given on a variety of goods and services to union members only. These programs are:

Union Members Discount Network (877-877-UMDN, www.umdn.com), a free discount program, offers savings at local and national businesses to all union members. UMDN has put together a "Local Network" of businesses (or "Preferred Providers") in New York that guarantees to give members discounts on the goods and services they provide. Preferred Providers include chiropractors, auto rentals, restaurants, pharmacies, dentists, beauty salons, personal trainers, legal services, tickets for concerts and sporting events, hotels, retail outlets, entertainment, opticians, and more. To become a UMDN member, simply click on the "Register" button at the top of the Home Page of their website and fill out the form, or call the toll-free number and register over the phone. To get your discount, just show the Preferred Provider your UMDN card (which will be sent to you within a few days of registering). You can obtain a list of Preferred Providers through the website or toll-free number. UMDN adds new Providers each week and extends "Bonuses" and "Freebies" to members for using the network.

Created in 1986 by the AFL-CIO, **Union Plus** (www.unionplus.org) provides union members and their families with valuable discounted consumer benefits. By using the collective purchasing power of more than thirteen million union members, Union Plus negotiates the best products and services at the lowest prices. Member benefits include discounts and deals on insurance, legal services, theme parks, movie tickets, cell phones, hotels, computers, vacation tours, car rentals, mortgages, credit cards, education services, entertainment and more. For more information and to register to utilize its discount services, visit the Union Plus website.

Members of Actors' Equity are eligible for benefits through **Working Advantage** (www.workingadvantage.com). This savings portal, created for the employees and members of thousands of companies, organizations and unions, offers discounts on myriad goods and services such as ski tickets, Broadway plays, movie tickets, video rentals, magazines, clothing, sporting events, theme parks, jewelry, household goods, gifts and gift certificates, online shopping, hotels, electronics, food and more. To become a member, go to the Working Advantage website, enter your Actors' Equity Association member ID number (775984141), contact information and e-mail address and password, which will be your username and password on the site. Once you are enrolled, you'll be eligible to access all of the Working Advantage deals and discounts. Working Advantage also maintains an incentive program in which, for registering and making purchases through the website, you are given "Advantage Points" that are redeemable for a variety of rewards.

🍎   🍎   🍎

Periodicals and Theater-Related Publications

The following is a compendium of what I feel is essential reading for actors. Unless otherwise noted, most can be found at libraries, as well as bookstores, newsstands and kiosks, and bookshops specializing in theater publications:

American Theatre Magazine, published by Theatre Communications Group, whose mission is to "offer a wide array of services... to strengthen, nurture and promote the professional not-for-profit theatre," is the definitive resource for actors wanting to stay current with both the New York and regional theater scene. Published monthly, *American Theatre* features in-depth news and analysis of the people, places and trends that are contributing to the vitality of the American theater. The magazine also includes essays and editorials on the health of the theater, theater facts and figures, and listings of current productions. Every fall, *American Theatre* publishes its "Season Preview," a detailed directory of plays set for the coming season of each TCG-affiliated company. A full script of a new play, usually produced by a TCG-member theater, appears every other month (often before publication in book form) within the pages of the magazine.

The practical and popular **Backstage** is virtually the only game in town when it comes to New York City casting weeklies. Besides its myriad audition notices—for everything from Broadway shows to off-off showcases, studio movies to student films, as well as commercials, industrials and extra-work—this paper covers all aspects of the entertainment business, including reviews, features about "the biz," industry news, theater and people profiles, thespian services, career chat, guides to shows in and around the metropolitan area, classifieds, teacher postings and obits. Of all the publications listed in this section, most seasoned theater professionals would almost certainly agree that *Backstage* is the most important resource for the new-to-New-York actor.

For me, **The New York Times (NYT)** is the mother of all newspapers. This venerable "paper of record," which has been reporting the news since the mid-nineteenth century, is the city's (and perhaps the country's) leading source for world, national and local news. The paper's coverage of the arts, food, real estate, books, science, culture, style, business and sports, as well as its editorial pages, are unsurpassed. As actors, being in touch with current events is vital to our art, our lives and our place in society, and there is no better way to be in touch than through the *Times*.

Of special interest to actors is the *NYT's* extensive daily articles on theatre and film, as well as reviews and listings. For the "starving artist" in each of us, the "Weekend Fine Arts/Leisure" section of the Friday edition of the newspaper offers a complete catalog of the coming weekend's free and inexpensive city activities. The column titled "Spare Times" lists everything from museum shows to walking tours, street fairs, free films, neighborhood festivals, fun runs, and bicycle tours as well as lots of stuff to do with kids. The pages also carry informative articles and full-length and capsule reviews of art gallery and museum exhibitions. It's a very handy guide to turn to, especially on those Fridays when you're whining in your apartment about not having plans for the weekend.

The mini-magazine **Ross Reports** is the leading guide to behind-the-scenes information for anyone in, or wanting to get into the film and television business. Each issue, which is updated monthly, contains complete listings of talent agents and agencies, casting directors, industry executives, production companies and facilities, studios and offices, daytime serials and prime-time series, talk and variety shows, talent unions, guilds and associations, and films in preparation and development. Each issue also features an article and contact information detailing a distinctive aspect of the business such as "Guide to Acting Schools and Coaches," "TV's Top 20 Casting Directors," "Animation and Voice-over Casting Directors," "Coming Clean on Casting Soaps," "In the Company of Screen Writers," and "Comedy Casting Guide." When sending out pictures and resumes or doing those vital publicity mailings, the *Ross Reports* is the best source for names and addresses to help connect you to "everybody who's anybody."

Show Business Weekly, the "original casting weekly of the performing arts," is chock-full of audition listings and trade information for New

York's up-and-coming legion of talent. *SBW* also contains news, features about plays and players, reviews of theater, film, CDs, videos and DVDs, and classifieds.

Theatre Directory, published annually by Theatre Communications Group, is an in-depth guide, including addresses, contact information, season dates, key personnel and union affiliation, to nonprofit professional theaters throughout the United States. The *Directory* also lists the myriad organizations and associations that serve both nonprofit theaters and individual theater artists.

Theatrical Index, the "voice of the theatre," is probably the most concise and all-encompassing guide to the New York theater scene available. This compact resource lists the shows "currently on the boards" both on and off-Broadway (including production and artistic credits), New York theatrical agencies, Broadway opening dates, shows scheduled to open, future off-Broadway plans, and a roster of all Broadway theaters with addresses. *Theatrical Index*'s "From the Regionals" section showcases select productions being done in the hinterlands, and its "Highlights" gives the behind-the-scenes lowdown on productions in New York and around the country. A word of warning: As great as this publication is, its $14 cost per month is hefty. *Theatrical Index* may be purchased at The Drama Book Shop; for subscriptions, contact Price Berkley Publishers—888 Eighth Avenue, New York, NY 10019—212-586-6343.

Variety, considered the "Bible" in "the business," is the best newsgathering and disseminating service for entertainment, advertising, publishing, and media professionals throughout the world. *Variety* reports breaking industry news, exclusive "scoops," box office numbers, theater ("legit" in *Variety* "slanguage") and film criticism, "who's who" and "who's where," obituaries, and production charts and data. Its "unmatched insider's perspective" on the latest development and trends in film, TV, music, legit, advertising, media and more make it indispensable for all performing artists.

SPECIAL OFFER

For readers of *An Actor Prepares . . . To Work in New York City*, Variety.com is offering an exclusive discount: You may subscribe to the webzine (same as the hardcopy version) for just $79 a year, a savings of $180 off the usual price of $259. For this special offer, go to www.variety.com/actorpreparesoffer.

The **Village Voice** a free, left-leaning newspaper hits the newsstands every Tuesday evening. The *Voice* carries exhaustive listings of most everything that is happening culturally in the city, some of the city's best and most thoughtful arts criticism, and even occasionally posts casting notices. Besides its comprehensive articles on everything from world, U.S. and New York City politics to music, art and theater, it is a veritable guide to everything cheap in New York. It is packed with discount coupons and ads for inexpensive stores and services, including futons, furniture, gyms, travel agents, electronics, cameras, mobile phones, music stores, opticians, clothing, restaurants, kung fu classes, even inexpensive doctors, dentists, liposuction and laser eye surgery. The *Voice's* Classifieds section is considered one of the best sources for finding an apartment in the city—not to mention a job, a "massage" or even a potential life partner!

The three city **weekly magazines—New York, The New Yorker,** and **Time Out New York**—all do a bang-up job of reporting on the city's art, politics, culture, dining, business, fashion, media and history, and carry exhaustive listings of most everything that is happening throughout the five boroughs. Although they all cover Gotham's best and brightest, each has a distinctive voice and varies greatly in tone and substance—the gossipy *New York Magazine* often does lifestyle articles and exposés of the "Art Dealer by Day, Hired Assassin by Night" genre; *The New Yorker's* raison d'être is in-depth analysis of world events, profound personality profiles, obscure poetry, lengthy fiction by literary lions, thoughtful arts criticism, and sophisticated (if sometimes impenetrable) cartoons. *Time Out New York* specializes in sound-bite-size articles on the hip and happening.

New York Magazine and *Time Out New York* are also indispensable for their weekly inventory of sales and bargains throughout the city. The categories vary widely, from clothing and accessories stores to food purveyors, gyms and health clubs, beauty spas, housewares and home emporiums, hair salons, opticians and even service businesses like dogwalkers, dry cleaners, personal shoppers and organizers, and house cleaning services. *New York Magazine Shops* published twice a year by

New York Magazine, not only lists the best stores in Manhattan, but also includes articles on sample sales, bargains and discounts.

Rehearsal Spaces

Need to rehearse a song, monologue or scene but your apartment's too small? Walls too thin? Neighbors complaining about you screeching "C'est Moi" from *Camelot* at all hours of the night? Below is a select inventory of the city's better rehearsal studio rentals, chosen for cleanliness, safety, privacy and affordability:

New York Spaces (www.newyorkspaces.com) has numerous clean, bright and spacious studios in three locations throughout the city, many ranging in price from $12 to $45 per hour. All of the rooms have windows and some are equipped with pianos and with phone lines for internet connections. You must call the New York Spaces central booking office at 212-799-5433 to reserve a room. Locations and hours are:

Eighth Avenue Studios
939 Eighth Avenue (between 55th and 56th Streets), Suite 307
212-397-1313
Monday—Friday, 9 A.M. to 11 P.M.
Saturday and Sunday, 10 A.M. to 9 P.M.

Ripley Grier Studios
520 Eighth Avenue (between 36th and 37th Streets), 16th Floor
212-643-9985
Monday—Friday, 9 A.M. to 11 P.M.
Saturday and Sunday, 10 A.M. to 11 P.M.

West 72nd Street Studios
131 West 72nd Street (between Broadway and Columbus Avenues), 2nd Floor
212-799-5433
Monday—Friday, 9 A.M. to 11 P.M.
Saturday and Sunday, 10 A.M. to 9 P.M.

Located in a landmark building in Chelsea, **Cap21 Studios** (18 West 18th Street, between Fifth and Sixth Avenues—212-807-0202, www.cap21.org) has many clean, well-lit and comfortable rooms at rates that won't break the bank. Cap21's smallest rooms start at $15 per hour; they do offer discounts to nonprofit organizations and companies. All rooms have pianos, the building is totally handicap accessible, and there are showers and changing rooms. To make reservations, contact the Facilities Manager at 212-807-0202. Hours of operation: Monday—Friday, 6:30 P.M. to 10:30 P.M.; Saturday and Sunday, 11 A.M. to 6 P.M.

Shetler Studios (939 Eighth Avenue, 3rd Floor—212-246-6655, www.shetlerstudios.com), located in the same building as New York Spaces' Eighth Avenue Studios in the heart of the theater district, maintains fifteen rehearsal rooms of various sizes that range in price from $15 to $38 an hour. The rooms are air-conditioned, have pianos and are handicapped accessible.

Responding to the dearth of affordable city rehearsal studios, one organization, **Exploring the Metropolis, Inc.** (www.xtmnyc.org), has stepped in to identify and create suitable rehearsal and performance spaces for actors, musicians and dancers. To achieve its goal of fostering "a vibrant and prolific performing arts community around shared resources of space and talent to increase stability and growth within the artistic community," the Exploring the Metropolis website maintains a free database of work space-related resources. The database, which is updated weekly, lists over 800 affordable rental spaces for rehearsal, recording and performance in a variety of professional venues as well as suitable locations in alternative facilities.

Restrooms

It was never my intention to include a chapter about bathrooms in New York, but as I shared my plans for this book with friends and colleagues, the overwhelming response was, "Tell us where there are toilets that are available to the public!"

We actors traverse every nook and cranny of this city in the pursuit of work, often in neighborhoods we know nothing about, and occasionally we need to use the facilities. You soon find that New York is bereft of public toilets and you have to be creative in your bathroom search. Some simple planning and logical sleuthing, however, will keep bladders empty, hair combed neatly and makeup perfectly applied.

The golden rule for gaining access to restrooms in restaurants, hotels and stores is never to ask if you may use the facilities. Only tourists ask, and the answer will always be "no." Pretend like you are a patron/guest and go for it. (Warning: No matter how badly you need to go, don't do as a friend of mine did and pee against a tree in Central Park. No sooner was his fly zipped than he was collared by two policemen and taken to jail. He spent forty harrowing hours becoming acquainted with the city's netherworld from which he was not allowed to use a phone for hours, so that neither his wife nor the theater company with which he was rehearsing a play—he was on his lunch break—knew where he was. He was fed bologna sandwiches for breakfast, lunch and dinner and never slept more than twenty minutes at a time.)

For me, the city's large **bookstores** have the best restrooms. In almost every part of Manhattan there is either a Barnes & Noble or Borders Books and the facilities in each are usually clean and not far from the front door. Best yet, you don't need a key and no one knows if you are there solely to use the waterworks or to buy books.

Barnes & Noble:
4 Astor Place at Broadway
396 Avenue of the Americas at 8th Street
33 East 17th Street at Union Square
105 Fifth Avenue at 18th Street
675 Sixth Avenue at 21st Street
901 Sixth Avenue at 22nd Street
385 Fifth Avenue at 54th Street
750 Third Avenue at East 47th Street
600 Fifth Avenue at 48th Street
160 East 54th Street at Third Avenue
1972 Broadway at 66th Street
2289 Broadway at 82nd Street

1280 Lexington Avenue at 86th Street
240 East 86th Street, between Second and Third Avenues

Borders Books:
461 Park Avenue at 57th Street
550 Second Avenue at 30th Street
100 Broadway near Wall Street
10 Columbus Circle

Most, if not all of the **fast food restaurants** like McDonald's, Burger King, Wendy's, Au Bon Pain, Ranch One, Boston Market and Popeye's have public facilities. Designated for "Customers Only" they often need a key to be opened. To gain entrance, act like a customer and pretend that you have just finished your happy meal. If it is obvious that you have not dined there and your need to go has reached emergency status, buy the cheapest thing on the menu and demand the damned key!

The first thing to do if you need to make a pit stop is look for a **hotel**. Almost all of Manhattan's neighborhoods have at least one medium to large hotel with public facilities located on or near the ground floor. None have a policing system to keep nonguests from using the facilities, so you won't be hassled, and in most the restrooms are impeccably clean.

Other **large retailers** like Kmart, Bed, Bath & Beyond, and Old Navy also have public restrooms.

Kmart:
One Pennsylvania Plaza on 34th Street at Seventh Avenue
770 Broadway at Astor Place

Bed, Bath & Beyond:
620 Avenue of the Americas at 19th Street
61st Street and First Avenue

Old Navy:
610 Avenue of the Americas at 18th Street
300 West 125th Street

150 West 34th Street, between Sixth and Seventh Avenues
503 Broadway, between Spring and Broome Streets

Manhattan's three **main transportation hubs** (Grand Central Terminal, Penn Station, and Port Authority Bus Terminal) all have toilets for the general public. The facilities at **Penn Station** (Seventh to Eighth Avenues between 30th and 32nd Streets) and **Grand Central** (42nd Street and Park Avenue) are large, clean, safe and centrally located. All I can say about the bathrooms at the **Port Authority** (Eighth to Ninth Avenues at 41st Street) is "yikes!" But, if you gotta go, you gotta go.

In each of the **major department stores**, there are at least a couple of men's and women's restrooms located on different floors. The larger the store, the more restrooms it has. These stores are scattered around three New York neighborhoods so that you are covered while you are in any of these areas:

Barney's—Madison Avenue at 61st Street
Henri Bendel—Fifth Avenue at 56th Street
Bergdorf Goodman—Fifth Avenue at 58th Street
Bloomingdale's—Lexington Avenue at 59th Street
Lord & Taylor—Fifth Avenue, between 38th and 39th Streets
Macy's—34th Street, between Sixth and Seventh Avenues
Saks Fifth Avenue—Fifth Avenue, between 49th and 50th
    Streets
Takashimaya—Fifth Avenue, between 49th and 50th Streets

In Midtown, where we do most of our auditioning, there are lots of bathroom options. The facilities in the **Actors' Equity Second Floor Members' Lounge** (165 West 46th Street) are the most convenient. If you wish to avoid a sea of people you know who will all want to tell you what they are up to and ask you the inevitable, "So, what are you doing?" stay away. Other bathrooms in the neighborhood are in the **Virgin Mega Store** on Broadway between 46th and 47th Streets in Times Square and several of the lower floors of the **Marriott Marquis Hotel** (across from the Virgin Mega Store). The beautiful and very trendy bathrooms at the **Paramount Hotel** (235 West 46th Street) are convenient at about forty yards from the hotel's front door and are a narcissist's wet dream—all mirrors, reflecting surfaces and low age-erasing lighting. **ESPN Zone** (4 Times Square, 42nd Street and Broadway) is the only place where, while sitting on the john, you may watch your favorite sports game. ESPN TV is screened on monitors right there in each stall.

Four of the city **parks** actually have public facilities. None will ever win awards for cleanliness, but they are convenient, safe and handy in times of need. You will find public park facilities in:

> **Washington Square Park**—Thompson Street at Washington Square
>
> **Tompkins Park**—Avenue A at 9th Street
>
> **Bryant Park**—Sixth Avenue, between 41st and 42nd Streets
>
> **Central Park**—Near the Delacorte Theatre at the West 81st Street entrance

Public and government buildings such as libraries, courthouses, unemployment offices and the like all have restrooms that are available to the public.

Most New Yorkers' favorite pastime is to grumble over the obscene number of **Starbucks** there are in this city. But complain as we may, Starbucks offers one great service to all New Yorkers: public restrooms. Since Starbucks is everywhere, we need never worry about finding a place to go. The next time you need to use a facility and don't know where one is, stop anyone on the street and ask for the nearest Starbucks. Ten to one there is one within spitting distance. The restrooms, of course, are for "Patrons Only" and may require a key. Have the attitude that you will be dropping a couple of gold bricks for a cup of joe just as soon as you "wash your hands" and you won't be hassled.

Resume Services

Intimidated about putting together a resume? If so, you can have the pros do it, for a price, at the following:

Professional Resumes, Inc.
60 East 42nd Street, Suite 839
New York, NY 10165
212-697-1282; 800-221-4425 (outside New York)
    For $150, Professional Resumes will create, layout and print your re-
sume (fifty copies are included in your order) on 8 x 10 paper. Changes
are "free" but you will be charged $32.50 for a stack of fifty copies of your
amended resume.

Shakespeare Mailing
312 West 36th Street, 2nd Floor
New York, NY 10018
212-560-8958
www.shakespearemailing.com
    For creating a resume, which includes consultation, layout and type-
setting, and posting with a photo on its website online (for two years),
Shakespeare Mailing charges $159. Changes cost $7 for one new credit
and $9 for up to five new credits.

Sheet Music

The following is a list of some of New York's best places to find sheet
music for auditions, repertoire, etc.:

Beethoven House Music
1841 Broadway
New York, NY 10023
212-757-8585
www.themusicstorenyc.com

CTI Records
88 University Place
New York, NY 10003
212-645-9302

Carl Fischer Inc.
65 Bleecker Street
New York, NY 10012
212-777-0900

Classical Vocal Reprints
3253 Cambridge Avenue
Riverdale, NY 10463-3618
718-601-1959
www.classicalvocalrep.com

Colony Records
1619 Broadway
New York, NY 10019
212-265-2050

Frank Music Company
250 West 54th Street
New York, NY 10019
212-582-1999

Half Price Music Shop
160 West 56th Street
New York, NY 10019
212-582-5840

Handy Brothers Music Company, Inc.
1697 Broadway
New York, NY 10019
212-247-0362

Joseph Patelson Music House
160 West 56th Street
New York, NY 10019
212-246-5633

Juilliard Bookstore
60 Lincoln Center Plaza
New York, NY 10023
212-799-5000

Lincoln Center Library for the Performing Arts (see section
on "Performing Arts Related Museums and Research
Institutions")
111 Amsterdam Avenue
New York, NY 10023
212-870-1630

Music Center Inc.
324 Canal Street
New York, NY 10013
212-343-2415

Sam Ash Music Store
160 West 48th Street
New York, NY 10036
212-398-6052

Tax Preparation

For over twenty-five years, **VITA (Volunteer Income Tax Assis-**
tance) has been offering free support to Actors' Equity, SAG and
AFTRA members in the preparation of their individual fed-
eral and state income tax returns. Located in the Actors' Equity   **BEST**
building (165 West 46th Street, 14th Floor—212-921-2548,   **BARGAIN**
www.actorsequity.org/services/tax.html), VITA is an Internal
Revenue Service program supported by the SAG and Equity Founda-
tions and the New York local of AFTRA. VITA volunteer tax preparers
are all fellow union members whom the IRS trains to assist in the preparation of basic tax returns.

During tax season (the first Monday in February through the last Friday in April), VITA's office is open Mondays, Wednesdays, Thursdays and Fridays from 11 A.M. to 5 P.M. It is best to make an appointment; go to the VITA office on Opening Day (the first Monday in February) with a paid-up union card. Otherwise, if you don't have an appointment, you can come in as a "walk-in," but you are attended to on a first-come/first-served basis. (Of the more than 1700 people who have their taxes prepared by VITA each season, only about 330 make appointments.) Whether or not you make an appointment, you must go to the VITA office in person, show your Equity, SAG or AFTRA card and pick up a packet of worksheets prior to having your taxes done.

VITA does offer year-round assistance to union members regarding income tax questions (provisions in contracts, etc.), those having trouble understanding IRS correspondence or who have been audited. Its off-season hours are July through January on Wednesdays only from 11 A.M. to 4 P.M.

VITA reminds all those who utilize its services that "since neither the volunteers nor their sponsoring unions receive remuneration for the service, they are not legally liable for the return in any way. Responsibility for the accuracy and completeness of the return rests solely with the person(s) filing the return. Should the return be audited by the I.R.S., there is no guarantee that the VITA volunteer who assisted in its preparation will be available for help."

If you are unwilling either to wait on the hours-long line at VITA on the first Monday in February or to risk not getting a first-come/first served appointment, **Marc Bernstein** (250 West 57th Street, Suite 2403—212-582-3133) is a great alternative. Marc has been in the business of actors' taxes for twenty-two years, during tax season writes a weekly column on the subject for *Backstage*, and prepares the returns of hundreds of actors each year. Unlike VITA, Marc's services are not gratis, but he charges fair prices and works miracles for all who utilize his services. A friend of mine says, "He's not dirt cheap, but I've used him for ten years and whether I've made no money or a lot of money (relatively speaking), he always saves me money." I've been a client of Marc's since 1984 and I've been so pleased with the work he's done for me that, if I could, I'd have the man canonized. Call early in the year for an appointment as he books up quickly. Fees are based on the complexity of the return.

For a good start to help yourself in preparing a tax return, check out CPA Peter Jason Riley's **The New Tax Guide for Artists of Every Persuasion** (Limelight Editions). This invaluable short reference book gives an overview of various types of income and expenses, and focuses on the deductions allowed by the IRS and the unique tax situations encountered by artists, including actors, singers, dancers, directors, visual artists, writers and musicians. Riley also details how performing artists can maximize deductions, reduce taxes, prepare for an audit, choose a tax advisor, set up a business entity and plan for retirement. Most helpful is the inclusion of spreadsheets for notating monthly and out-of-town expenses, earned income and claimed exemptions. As Riley says, the goal of his book is to help "make the tax preparation process less onerous and most importantly SAVE TAX DOLLARS!" (Note: This book is tax-deductible!)

Tax Write-offs

I'm no longer surprised by the number of actors, especially those fresh out of acting school, who know little or nothing about their income taxes, deductions, or even filing a claim. Consequently, I've been saying for years that every actor-training program in the nation should offer a "Business of 'Show Business' " course to discuss tax matters. We actors need to have a clear understanding of the income tax deductions we are entitled to *and how to take them*, because we can significantly reduce our tax burden and perhaps save ourselves hundreds, even thousands, of dollars annually.

An income tax deduction is the amount the government allows us to subtract from our overall annual tax bill. These deductions are calculated from the dollars we spend looking for work and marketing ourselves, but may include our out-of-town expenses, traditional IRA contributions, union dues, and charitable donations among many others.

A comprehensive list follows of the deductions actors are usually eligible to take. Be diligent and disciplined in keeping records, saving receipts, and logging daily business expenses in a journal, and you can save more money. But also, find a tax person who specializes in actors' taxes, because that person will have an understanding of the many and varied deductions we are allowed and knows how to navigate the individual tax rules and regulations of all fifty states (remember we work all over the country); it is almost always more financially advantageous to hire a tax preparer than to do it yourself or have them done at a tax assembly line outfit like H&R Block.

Usual Write-offs:

- **Accompanist and Audition Expenses**

- **Advertising and Publicity**—head shots, resumes, guides like the *Players' Guide* or *Academy Players Directory,* promotional theater tickets for agents, producers and directors for plays that you are in.

- **Agents' Commissions and Manager's Fees**

- **Alimony**

- **Answering Service**

- **Audio/Video Equipment**

- **Blank Video/Audio Tapes to Record Programs for Research**

- **Books (Research)**—including this book!

- **Cable, Studio and Equipment Rental**

- **Cable TV**

- **CD's, Videos and Audio Tapes (Research)**—purchase and rental

- **Charitable Contributions**—monetary contributions, donations of items other than cash or checks (e.g., clothing, books, furniture, etc.— for these donations, you must get a receipt from the charitable organization if the value of the donation exceeds $500 and provide a photocopy of the receipt for the IRS).

- **Child and Dependent Care**—the amount incurred by you and your spouse for such care so that you can work or look for work. The I.R.S. requires the social security number or employer ID number for each individual or childcare facility employed.

- **Coaching, Classes and Lessons**

- **Computer Services**—cost of computer services to create documents such as resumes, mailing labels, marketing materials, etc.

- **Dancewear and Costumes/Wardrobe**—for clothing items used solely for theatrical purposes (e.g. a clown costume, a Renaissance costume), and that cannot be considered as "street clothing." (Note: You need to prove this in case of an audit.)

- **Equipment Repairs and Maintenance**—cost of repairs and maintenance of equipment like televisions, VCRs, computers, tape recorders, CD players, stereos and DVD players.

- **Gifts for People in the Business**—a maximum of $25 per person per year

- **Home Office**

- **Medical Expenses**—only Unreimbursed Medical Expenses and Health Insurance Premiums. For this deduction, you must show that you spent a certain percentage of your annual income on this category.

- **Monthly Internet Connection** (Research and Promotion)

- **Mortgage Interest**—the amount of interest you paid on your mortgage. For co-ops, this includes the amount of maintenance deemed deductible as interest by the co-op board. Co-op owners can enter the number of shares they own.

- **Musical Arrangements**

- **Office Supplies, Stationery and Postage**

- **Pager or Beeper Service**

- **Piano Tuning**

- **Professional, Legal or Copyright Fees**

- **Professional Makeup, Wigs and Hair Care**—show that these items are used solely for performing purposes.

- **Real Estate Tax**—if you own a home, condominium or co-op, the amount of real estate tax you pay. For co-op owners, this includes the amount of maintenance the co-op board deems deductible as real estate tax.

- **Rehearsal Studio Rental**

- **Restaurant Entertaining**—"wining and dining" of performing arts professionals such as directors, agents, casting people, etc.

- **Scripts, Scores and Plays**

- **Student Loan Interest**

- **Tax Preparation**

- **Telephone**—business long distance, pay phone calls, percentage of business-related cell phone calls, percentage of home phone.

- **Theatrical Props**—you must show that this purchase or rental was solely for theatrical use.

- **Tickets for Viewing Theater and Film (Research)**

- **Tips and Gratuities**—to dressers, hair and makeup people, theater doormen, etc.

- **Trade Publications**—*Backstage, American Theatre, Daily* and *Weekly Variety, Ross Reports*, etc.

- **Traditional IRA Contribution**—Up to $3,000 contribution annually is tax-free provided your earnings did not exceed a federally prescribed amount. (Note: The prescribed maximums change yearly, so consult your tax person before contributing.)

- **Transportation for Seeking Employment**—includes taxis, subways, buses, etc.

- **Travel Expenses for Out-of-Town Auditions**—transportation, lodging, auto rental and gas, food, laundry and dry cleaning, local transportation, local telephone and long-distance business calls. If you use your own car, list the total mileage accrued during the business part of your trip.

- **Travel Expenses Incurred While Working Out-of-Town**—transportation, lodging, auto rental and gas, food, laundry and dry cleaning, local transportation, local telephone and long-distance business calls. If you use your own car, list the total mileage accrued during your business trip.

- **Union Dues**—basic dues, initiation fees and 2 percent assessment to Actors' Equity Association.

- Video Tape Rentals

Training Institutions

The following is a partial list, impartially assembled alphabetically, of several of the city's premier actor training institutions:

Acting

The Acting Studio
P.O. Box 230389
New York, NY 10023
212-580-6600

The Actors Center
12 West 27th Street
New York, NY 10001
212-447-6309

Actors Connection
630 Ninth Avenue
New York, NY 10036
212-977-6666

The Actors Institute
159 West 25th Street, 9th Floor
New York, NY 10001
212-924-8888

The Actors Theatre Workshop, Inc.
145 West 28th Street, 3rd Floor
New York, NY 10001
212-947-1386

American Academy of Dramatic Arts
120 Madison Avenue
New York, NY 10016
212-686-9244

American Musical & Dramatic Academy
2109 Broadway
New York, NY 10023
212-787-5300

Atlantic Theater Company Acting School
453 West 16th Street
New York, NY 10011
212-691-5919

Circle in the Square Theatre School
1633 Broadway
New York, NY 10019
212-307-0388

Creative Acting Company
122 West 26th Street, Suite 1102
New York, NY 10001
212-352-2103

Gene Frankel Theatre & Film Workshop
24 Bond Street
New York, NY 10012
212-777-1767

HB Studios
120 Bank Street
New York, NY 10014
212-675-2370

Jim Bonney Acting Training
134 West 26th Street
New York, NY 10001
212-352-3327

Kimball Studios
60 East 13th Street, Suite 3W
New York, NY 10003
212-260-6373

Lee Strasberg Institute
115 East 15th Street
New York, NY 10003
212-533-5500

Maggie Flanigan Studio
153 West 27th Street
New York, NY 10001
917-606-0982

Michael Howard Studios
152 West 25th Street
New York, NY 10001
212-645-1526

Neighborhood Playhouse
340 East 54th Street
New York, NY 10022
212-688-3770

New Actors' Workshop
259 West 30th Street, 2nd Floor
New York, NY 10001
212-947-1310

New York Film Academy
100 East 17th Street
New York, NY 10003
212-674-4300

Caymichael Patten Studio
211 West 61st Street
New York, NY 10023
212-765-7021

Paul Mann Actors Workshop
215 West 90th Street
New York, NY 10024
212-877-8575

Penny Templeton Studio
261 West 35th Street
New York, NY 10001
212-643-2614

Sande Shurin Acting Studio and Theatre
311 West 43rd Street
New York, NY 10036
212-262-6848

School for Film and Television
39 West 19th Street, 12th Floor
New York, NY 10011
212-645-0030

Stella Adler Studio
419 Lafayette Street
New York, NY 10003
800-270-6775

Terry Schreiber Studio
151 West 26th Street, 7th Floor
New York, NY 10001
212-741-0209

The Theatre Studio
750 Eighth Avenue
New York, NY 10036
212-719-0500

TVI Actors Studio
165 West 46th Street, Suite 509
New York, NY 10036
212-302-1900

Ward Studio
145 West 28th Street, Suite 8F
New York, NY 10001
212-239-1456

Weist Barron Studios
35 West 45th Street, 6th Floor
New York, NY 10036
212-840-7025

William Esper Studio
261 West 35th Street
New York, NY 10001
212-904-1350

Dance and Movement

Actors Movement Studio
302 West 37th Street
New York, NY 10018
212-736-3309

Broadway Dance Center
221 West 57th Street, 5th Floor
New York, NY 10023
212-582-9304

Peridance
132 Fourth Avenue
New York, NY 10003
212-505-0886

Steps on Broadway
2121 Broadway, 2nd Floor
New York, NY 10023
212-874-2410

Singing

Singers Forum
39 West 19th Street, 4th Floor
New York, NY 10011
212-366-0541

Voice and Speech

VoicePresence Training Consultancy
119 West 72nd Street, Suite 338
New York, NY 10023
646-286-5180

Websites

The following is a list of performing arts related websites, each categorized according to genre:

Actor Union, Guild and Organization Sites
www.actorsequity.org (Actors' Equity)
www.afm.org (American Federation of Musicians)
www.aftra.org (American Federation of Television and Radio Artists)
www.atpam.org (Association of Theatrical Press Agents and Managers)
www.directorsguild.org (Directors Guild of America)
www.dramatistsguild.org (Dramatists Guild of America)
www.hellohola.org (Hispanic Organization of Latin Actors)
www.iatse-intl.org (International Alliance of Theatrical Stage Employees)
www.naatco.org (National Asian American Theatre Co.)
www.nygiaa.org (Guild of Italian American Actors)
www.sag.org (Screen Actors Guild)
www.ssdc.org (Society of Stage Directors and Choreographers)
www.theatrewomen.org (League of Professional Theatre Women)

www.usa829.org (United Scenic Artists)
www.wgaeast.org (Writers Guild of America)

Audition and Actor Resource and Reference Sites

www.acadpd.org (The Academy Players Directory)
www.actingbiz.com (Actor Resource)
www.actingdepot.com (Actor Resource)
www.actorpoint.com (Actor Resource)
www.actorscraft.com (Actor Resource)
www.actorsfcu.org (Actors Federal Credit Union)
www.actorsfund.org (Actors' Fund of America)
www.actorsny.com (Actor Resource)
www.actorsource.com (Actor Resource)
www.alluringimages.com (Photo Reproduction)
www.oscars.org (Academy of Motion Picture Arts and Sciences)
www.artistscommunityfcu.org (Credit Union)
www.backstage.com (Casting/Actor Resource)
www.bcefa.org (Broadway Cares/Equity Fights AIDS)
www.bl.uk/collections/sound-archive/accents.html (British Library
    Sound Archive)
www.breakdownservices.com (Casting)
www.careertransition.org (Career Transition for Dancers)
www.caryn.com/acting (Acting Resource)
www.castinglist.com (Casting)
www.castingsociety.com (Casting Society of America)
www.equityleague.org (Equity League Pension, Health and 401k Trust
    Funds)
www.fullmoonnyc.com (Demo Editing)
www.hendersonenterprises.com (Mailing labels)
www.ibdb.com (Internet Broadway Database)
www.imdb.com (Internet Movie Database)
www.lortel.org (Internet Off-Broadway Database)
www.nephotoanddesign.com (Photo Reproduction)
www.ntcp.org (Non-Traditional Casting Project)
www.nypl.org (New York Public Library)
www.onstage.org (Actor Resource)

www.players-guide.com (Players' Guide)
www.precisionphotos.com (Photo Reproduction)
www.prolabels.com (Mailing Labels)
www.redbirdstudio.com/AWOL/acting2.html (Actor Resource)
www.redwallproductions.com (Workshop Films)
www.reproductions.com (Photo Reproduction)
www.showbusinessweekly.com (Casting/Actor Resource)
www.spotlightcd.com (Casting)
www.stagemanagers.org (Stage Managers' Association)
www.tarantolabs.com (Photo Reproduction)
www.theatredb.com (Internet Theatre Database)
www.theatre-link.com (Theater Information)
www.ukans.edu/~idea/ (International Dialects of English Archive)
www.vasta.org (Voice and Speech Trainers Association)
www.xtmnyc.org (Exploring the Metropolis—Rehearsal Spaces)

News, Reviews and Culture Sites
www.aislesay.com (Theater Reviews and Opinion)
www.allianceforarts.org (Arts Information)
www.allny.com (New York City Information)
www.americantheatreweb.com (Theater Information)
www.anactorpreparesnyc.com (NYC Information/Actor Resource)
www.botz.com/nytheatre (Theater News and Criticism)
www.broadway.com (Theater News/Information)
www.broadwaybeat.com (Theater News/Information)
www.broadwaystars.com (Theater News/Information)
www.broadwayworld.com (Theater News/Information)
www.curtainup.com (Theater News/Information)
www.entertainment-link.com (Theater Tickets)
www.fieldtrip.com/ny/index_ny.htm (New York Theater Information)
www.ilovenytheatre.com (Theater Information)
www.livebroadway.com (Theater News/Information)
www.moviefone.com (Movie Tickets)
www.musicalheaven.com (Theater Information)
www.newyork.citysearch.com (New York City Information)
www.newyorkmag.com (New York Magazine)

www.notfortourists.com (New York City Information)
www.ny.com (New York City Information)
www.nyc.com (New York City Information)
www.nyc.gov (New York City Information)
www.nycpulse.com (New York City Information)
www.nyctourist.com (New York City Information)
www.nytheatre.com (Theater Information)
www.nytheatre-wire.com (Theater News/Information)
www.nytimes.com (New York Times)
www.offbroadway.com (Theater Information)
www.oobr.com (Off-Off-Broadway Reviews)
www.papermag.com (Paper Magazine)
www.playbill.com (Playbill Magazine)
www.readio.com (New York City Information)
www.showpeople.com (Show People Magazine)
www.avant-rus.com/stagebill/level-2/about.html (Stagebill Magazine)
www.talkentertainment.com (Film/Television Information)
www.talkinbroadway.com (Theater Information)
www.tcg.org (Theatre Communications Group)
www.tdf.org (Theatre Development Fund)
www.theatermania.com (Theater Information)
www.theatrereviews.com (Theater Reviews)
www.theinsider.com/nyc (New York City Information)
www.things2doinnewyork.com (New York City Information)
www.thingstodo.com/states/NY/nyc (New York City Information)
www.timeoutny.com (Time Out Magazine)
www.tonyawards.com (Tony Awards)
www.totaltheater.com (Theater Information)
www.variety.com (Daily Variety)
www.villagevoice.com (Village Voice)

Glossary of Words and Phrases

The following is a glossary of acting related words, phrases, and lingo used by "the business." Like the jargon geared to any other profession, to be successful, it is essential that actors become familiar with this terminology:

Action   What a character does to achieve an "objective." Also, the word a film or television director says to cue an actor to act; the opposite of "cut."

Activities   The physical things an actor does in performance. Same as "business."

Ad lib   Improvised, spontaneous material or response performed without the benefit of rehearsal. Same as "improvisation."

Adjustment   A change in action or character trait an actor makes to fit the changing circumstances of a scene; often given by a director.

Affective memory   An actor's exploration and/or re-creation of a past event in his or her life so that it can be used in the development of a character.

Agent   A person who represents an actor to the industry. The agent represents his or her clients' interests by submitting them for work to casting directors and negotiating contracts with theater, film and television companies.

Air date   The day on which a specific commercial or television program will be broadcast.

Antagonist   The villain of a dramatic piece. Is often the "obstacle" to the goals the hero or protagonist is trying to achieve.

Antihero   A protagonist who has qualities or eccentricities not usually associated with heroes.

Audience   Those watching a performance, be they in a theater, movie house or at home sitting on their couch with a remote control and a bottle of Thunderbird.

Audition A short performance, done before agents or potential employers, by actors who are seeking employment.

Background A small, nonspeaking part usually seen only fleetingly on camera, if at all. Same as "extra."

Backstage Any area behind the scene of action on the set that does not appear to an audience.

Beat A unit of text in a scene denoting the end of an action; usually has a beginning, a middle and an end. A mini scene within a scene. If a play is made up of many scenes, a scene is comprised of many beats.

Billing Screen credits (i.e. "co-star," "featured," "principal," "day-player," "under-five," etc.) given to film and television actors according to the terms of their contracts.

Bit part A small part with only a few lines.

Blocking The physical arrangement and movement by an actor on a set.

Breakdown Services An online publication transmitted each weekday to agents and managers via the internet with information about acting roles that are soon to be cast. Agents and managers peruse the breakdowns, determine who from their roster would be appropriate for each role and submit those actors to the corresponding casting director.

Business The physical action used by an actor to add dimension to his or her characterization, scene or shot.

Buyout Payment to an actor in a commercial on a single-performance basis without "use-fees."

Call A timetable, either published, posted or telephoned, in which actors are instructed when to show up for a performance, rehearsal or audition.

Callback A request for an actor to repeat an audition. A second opportunity for an actor to vie for a role.

Cast All the performers in a play, film or television show.

Casting director   The person who assists a director in casting a project. His or her job is to set up appointments for actors, book the audition space, inform actors who have been cast and be knowledgeable about the talent pool.

Cattle Call   A general audition in which anyone may attend. Also known as an "open call."

Character   The person the actor plays.

Character actor   A versatile actor who can play a variety of roles; usually not a principal role but often a juicier one.

Choices   The qualities an actor incorporates in his or her portrayal of a character; the actions an actor chooses to pursue his or her objective.

Class A spot   A commercial that sponsors a television program on a "network" and plays in twenty or more cities. Typically the most remunerative category of commercial spot.

Client   The company that is paying to have a commercial spot produced.

Cold Reading   An audition in which an actor reads aloud from a script with little or no rehearsal beforehand. The majority of film, television and commercial auditions are cold readings.

Comedy   A film, theater piece or television show intended to amuse an audience.

Comedy of manners   A comedy that mocks the social behaviors of the characters it presents.

Commercial   A broadcast advertisement designed to sell a product.

Comp card   A marketing tool used by both photographers and models. It is a lithographed card, usually the size of a headshot, which contains several examples of either's work.

Contact sheet   A page containing miniature versions of all the shots taken during a headshot photo session.

Contract   A written agreement between an employer and an employee (i.e. theater and actor), between an actor and his or her representation, or between management and union with stated terms concerning salary, schedules and conditions.

Copy The dialogue spoken by actors in a commercial.

Co-star A large role on a TV show or in a film that is not the lead; usually a guest star.

Craft The mastered skills and techniques an actor uses to develop and enhance artistic talent.

Cue The last words of a speech or end of an action that prompts another actor to act, speak, execute stage business, etc. Also, a film/television term meaning the signal to start.

Cue card A large, off-camera card on which a performer's script is written. Same as "idiot card."

Cut The word used by a director to tell an actor to stop acting. The opposite of "action."

Day-player A principal role played by a guest actor for one to several days in a film, soap or TV show.

Demo reel A VHS or DVD copy of snippets of the best moments of an actor's work on film, television and commercials. It is used to market talent, type and range to anyone who can help actors get work.

Dialogue The lines spoken by characters in any dramatic medium.

Double To play more than one role in a single play.

Drama A performance by actors for presentation to an audience. Also, a performed piece showing the protagonist engaged in extraordinary conflict while pursuing an objective, usually with strong emotional impact arising from a crisis.

Emotional recall An actor's evocation of a past emotion or experience from his or her life to be applied to the character being portrayed.

Extra Small, nonspeaking role. Often appears in crowd scenes. The same as "background."

Featured role The same as a "co-star."

Feature film   A full-length film meant to be commercially exhibited in theaters.

Feedback   The information given to an agent by a casting director regarding his or her client's performance in an audition.

Fourth Wall   The implied wall through which the audience watches a performance. In the theater it encompasses the opening in the proscenium; in film and television it is the camera lens.

Freelancing   When an actor either represents himself/herself, or works with one or more agents without being signed exclusively.

From the top   A term used in rehearsals meaning to repeat a scene from the beginning.

Given circumstances   The events and information of any play, film or television show, established by the writer, that affects what a character does.

Goal   What a character wants; a character's "objective."

Golden time   Sundays, holidays, or other special occasions on which union members work and are paid more than overtime wages, often time and a half.

Green room   The off-stage area where actors wait until called to appear onstage or in front of the camera.

Hero   The principal performer of a dramatic piece. He or she has an objective, performs various actions to achieve his or her goal and confronts obstacles in that pursuit. Same as "protagonist."

Homework   The character work an actor does before a rehearsal, performance, class or audition.

Idiot card   A large off-camera card in which a performer's script is written. Same as "cue card."

Improvisation   An unrehearsed, spontaneous scene, in which an actor uses his or her own words and business. Same as "ad lib."

Industrial film   A film designed to present selected information about a large industrial enterprise like financial institutions or pharmaceutical companies. These can also be in-house training films for corporations for the purpose of teaching employees company procedures, rules, etc.

Instrument The actor himself/herself.

Intention What a character intends to do. The reason a character performs an action.

Justification The process utilized by an actor to believe in or to "justify" the reality of each of his or her character's actions.

Lead role Starring role.

Line Reading How a line is said. Also, instruction on how to say a line.

Lines Dialogue spoken by a performer.

Magic if A term coined by director/teacher/father of the Method Constantin Stanislavski to describe the action by which an actor places him/herself into the given circumstances of a scene. Example: "What 'if' my uncle murdered my father and married my mother? How would I feel? Behave?"

Manager A person who manages an actor's career. The manager's duties include acting as an intermediary between the actor and agent, introducing actors to agents (and firing an agent if need be), and seeking work for his or her client. For their services, managers receive anywhere from 15 to 20 percent of an actor's salary. Unlike agents, managers are not licensed or franchised by the unions and are therefore forbidden to negotiate contracts.

Mannerisms Physical behavior that enhances the uniqueness of a character. Includes quirks, tics, traits, habits, vocal pattern and timbre, comportment, etc.

Mark Term used in film and television to denote the place where an actor must stand or arrive at in each shot. It is usually a tape or chalk mark placed on the studio floor.

Miscast Referring to an actor who has been cast in a role for which he or she is not suited.

Moment to moment Living in the present from one "beat" to the next.

Monologue   A speech from a play, film or television script spoken by one actor as part of a scene. Usually performed by an actor in an audition for an agent or others who want to see what the actor can do.

Mugging   Exaggerated facial gestures designed to entertain an audience at the expense of playing a part, scene, or moment truthfully.

Network   One of the four leading television broadcasters: ABC, CBS, Fox and NBC

Notes   Adjustments and critique given by a director.

Objective   The character's goal. What a character wants.

Obstacle   The physical, moral, psychological impediments preventing a character from achieving his or her goal.

Open call   A general audition in which anyone may attend. Also known as a "cattle call."

Preparation   What an actor does prior to a performance or audition so that he or she may be propelled into either with a fully realized character.

Prior circumstances   The events of the play that occur before the play or a particular scene, that affect what a character does.

Producer   The person who oversees all financial and artistic aspects of a film, television show, commercial or theatrical endeavor.

Props   The objects an actor handles.

Protagonist   The principal performer of a dramatic piece. He or she has an objective, performs various actions to achieve his or her goals and confronts obstacles in that pursuit. Same as "hero."

Reader   The person hired by a casting director to read with actors who are auditioning.

Recurring role   A character that is featured on a few to several episodes of a regular television show.

Rehearsal   The process of readying a play or audition for presentation by exploration and repetition.

Relationship The connection of a character to others in a play, film or TV program.

Residuals Earnings by performers, in addition to their salaries, from television programs after the initial airing.

Scale The minimum union rates paid to television, commercial and industrial film actors.

Scale plus ten "Scale" pay plus an extra ten percent that is to be paid to the actor's agent.

Screen test An audition by actors in which cameras and sound equipment are used.

Sense memory An actor's re-creation of an experience through the memory of the five senses from his or her life so that he or she may play a truthful sensory response. I.e., memory that allows an actor to convincingly say as his or her character, "Those flowers smell beautiful," in a play in which the prop flowers are plastic.

Showcase The presentation of a play or series of one-acts or scenes, usually in out of the way and/or down-scale venues, to present the talents of theater artists to potential future employers, and those who can help them find work.

Sides A part of a script, usually a short scene, used for an audition.

Signed client An actor who is signed exclusively to an agent for representation.

Sitcom Situation comedy—a television comedy series in which the same characters appear regularly and are involved in comic situations that arise from their relationships and environments.

Slapstick Comic acting that focuses on violent or exaggerated behavior and actions.

Slate Stating your name (and sometimes agency) before beginning a videotaped audition.

Soap Opera A melodramatic television series, airing daily Monday to Friday, that is named for the soap manufacturers (like Proctor and

Gamble) who routinely sponsored them from their inception in the early days of radio and television to the present.

Spine   Same as a "through line."

Storyboard   A set of sketches, arranged in sequence on panels, outlining the scenes that make up the story of a film, TV show or commercial.

Subtext   The real meaning under the text. The intentions and reality behind what a character says.

Super objective   A character's main objective throughout a play, film or television show.

Taft-Hartley Act   A law that allows non-union actors to work up to 30 days on his or her *first* union production without having to join the union.

Talent   A performer or performers.

Talent agency   An agency that markets the talents and negotiates the contracts of the performers it represents.

Talent union   A labor union to which professional performers belong.

Through line   The active execution of the "super objective" in a play, film or television show. What the actor/character does throughout the entire course of a role that helps him or her achieve the super objective.

Tragedy   A drama in which the principal character or characters experience profound suffering and inner conflict, usually ending in death or disaster.

Transition   The change or shift from the end of one "beat" to the beginning of another.

Truth   The expression of actions that is realistic.

Type   The categorizing of actors by appearance according to the roles in which they are apt to be cast.

Under-five   An actor in a soap who has five lines or less of dialogue. Not to be confused with "extra" or "bit part."

Understudy A performer who substitutes, when necessary (i.e., for illness, vacation, etc.) for a principal performer, having learned all of the role's dialogue and action.

Union signatory A producer or production company that has signed an agreement with one or more acting unions pledging to employ union members.

Use-fees "Residuals" for work in commercials.

Voice-over In film or television, the voice that speaks while a picture or scene is being shown. This is usually narration or a voice regaling the virtues of the product being showcased.

Walk-on A small part, usually with few or no lines. Same as a "bit part."

Wild spot A non-network commercial that airs during a local station break. Instead of "use-fees," the compensation for an actor in a wild spot, no matter how often the spot runs, is a flat fee paid in 13-week cycles.

Wrap A term used in film, TV and commercials to denote the successful completion of a shot or the end of the shooting day.

About the Author

Craig Wroe is an actor, writer and teacher who has lived in New York City since 1984. His acting credits include appearances on London's West End and the Bristol Old Vic, off- and off-off-Broadway, film, television, commercials, industrials and several leading regional theaters. As a teacher, Craig lectures on acting and "the business" at colleges and universities throughout the country and is on the faculty of New York's School for Film and Television. As author of the highly successful *An Actor Prepares . . . to Live in New York City* (Limelight Editions, 2003), Craig has conducted seminars on "Living the Good Life in the Big Apple" for the Learning Annex, and appeared on NBC's *Weekend Today in New York*.